The Way It Is

William Stafford's last poem, (reduced)
from the Daily Writings, 28 August 1993 (see page 46)

The Way It Is

NEW & SELECTED POEMS BY

William Stafford

GRAYWOLF
PRESS

Publication of this volume is made possible in part by a grant provided by the Minnesota State Arts Board through an appropriation by the Minnesota State Legislature, and by a grant from the National Endowment for the Arts. Significant support has also been provided by Dayton's, Mervyn's, and Target stores through the Dayton Hudson Foundation, the Andrew W. Mellon Foundation, the McKnight Foundation, the General Mills Foundation, the St. Paul Companies, and other generous contributions from foundations, corporations, and individuals. To these organizations and individuals we offer our heartfelt thanks.

Published by Graywolf Press
2402 University Avenue, Suite 203
Saint Paul, Minnesota 55114
All rights reserved.

www.graywolfpress.org

Published in the United States of America

ISBN 1-55597- 269-1

2 4 6 8 9 7 5 3 1
First Graywolf Printing, 1998

Library of Congress Catalog Card Number: 97-80082

Cover photograph: Bruce Heinemann, "Waterdrops on Leaves," from the book, *The Art of Nature: Reflections on the Grand Design*, 1993

Cover design: Tree Swenson

Many of the poems in this volume were previously published in *Stories That Could Be True* (Harper & Row, 1977); *Things That Happen Where There Aren't Any People* (BOA Editions, 1980); *Wyoming Circuit* (Tideline Press, 1980); *A Glass Face in the Rain* (Harper & Row, 1982); *Roving Across Fields* (Barnwood Press Cooperative, 1983); *Segues*, with Marvin Bell (David R. Godine, 1983); *Smoke's Way* (Graywolf Press, 1983); *Listening Deep* (Penmaen Press, 1984); *You Must Revise Your Life* (University of Michigan Press, 1986); *An Oregon Message* (Harper & Row, 1987); *Annie-Over*, with Marvin Bell (Honeybrook Press, 1988); *Kansas Poems* (Woodley Memorial Press, 1990); *Passwords* (HarperPerennial, 1991); *The Long Sigh the Wind Makes* (Adrienne Lee Press, 1991); *Getting the Knack*, with Stephen Dunning (National Council of Teachers of English, 1992); *My Name Is William Tell* (Confluence Press, 1992); *Who Are You Really, Wanderer?* (Honeybrook Press, 1993); *The Darkness Around Us Is Deep* (HarperPerennial, 1993); *Even in Quiet Places* (Confluence Press, 1996); *Crossing Unmarked Snow* (University of Michigan Press, 1998).

Grateful acknowledgment is made to the editors of the following publications, in which many of the poems in Part I of this book first appeared: *After the Storm: A Gulf War Anthology; The American Scholar; Artworks* (Portland Metropolitan Arts Commission); *Bakunin; Border and Boundaries* (Blue Heron Publishing); *Canto; Chadakoin Review; Cream City Review; The Fair; The Georgia Review; Harmonika* (Vienna); *The Hungry Mind Review; Left Bank; Light; Michigan Quarterly Review; Motes; The Nation; New Myths; The New Yorker; Nimrod; Poetry; Sequoia; Southern Review; Tar River Poetry; Virginia Quarterly Review; West Wind Review.*

Contents

There's a Thread You Follow (Poems written in 1993)

Stories That Could Be True

FROM *Stories That Could Be True* (1977)

FROM *West of Your City* (1960)

FROM *Traveling through the Dark* (1962)

FROM *The Rescued Year* (1966)

FROM *Allegiances* (1970)

Someday, Maybe (1973)

Why the Sun Comes Up

FROM Smoke's Way (1983)

Selections from other volumes (1980–93)

How These Words Happened

FROM *A Glass Face in the Rain* (1982)

FROM *An Oregon Message* (1987)

FROM *Passwords* (1991)

Preface

IN OUR TIME there has been no poet who revived human hearts and spirits more convincingly than William Stafford. There has been no one who gave more courage to a journey with words, and silence, and an awakening life.

Rarely has a voice felt so intimate and so collective at once. How did he do this? An intense awareness of presence and absence permeates here. He embraced and saluted the process of working. He meandered, and valued the turns. He honored, while demystifying anything that rang of pomp. He dug in the ground. He picked things up and looked at them. He had so many frequent flier miles he could have started his own program. He answered people's letters diligently, often closing with "Adios."

He sent poems to people who asked for them. No magazine was too small for his consideration. He was marvelously funny, with a wry tip of wit, the folded poems coming out of one pocket, going back to the other. He left devotees in his wake but wouldn't have thought of them that way. He befriended the earth and its citizens most generously and attentively, at the same time remaining solitary in his countenance, intact, composed, mysterious, complete in his humble service.

There was, in William Stafford and his poetry, a profoundly refreshing, elemental life force which accepted good surprise and failure, exaltation and stumbling, with nearly equal regard.

There was, in William Stafford, a vast and necessary oxygen. If you were fortunate to encounter him in a reading hall or backwoods cabin, in a classroom or library or cafe, at the Library of Congress or on a beach, you could feel the larger air of his voice overtaking you very quickly. It was heartening, congenial, and utterly unpredictable.

If you discover his voice for the first time here, trust that his spoken voice travels through the poems indelibly. Sometimes we, the readers, feel we are coming from inside his poems. If you read them many times over, aloud to yourself, slowly and carefully, savoring the pauses, you will hear. It has not left us.

William Stafford, originally from the land of Kansas, to the land of Oregon, to the widest lands of being, was a champion of language, a seeker, a deep rememberer, a purely original poet, and a beloved man. Now fiercely missed. But read these poems. That is part of it.

NAOMI SHIHAB NYE
San Antonio
September 1997

My dreams feel right. They get away but leave a sense of—
"Yes. That's the way it is."

WILLIAM STAFFORD
Daily Writings,
14 July 1993

The Way It Is

NEW POEMS

Sometimes I Breathe (1992)

There's a Thread You Follow
(Poems written in 1993)

Sometimes I Breathe (1992)

Sky

I like you with nothing. Are you
what I was? What I will be?
I look out there by the hour,
so clear, so sure. I could
smile, or frown—still nothing.

Be my father, be my mother,
great sleep of blue; reach
far within me; open doors,
find whatever is hiding; invite it
for many clear days in the sun.

When I turn away I know
you are there. We won't forget
each other: every look is a promise.
Others can't tell what you say
when it's the blue voice, when
you come to the window and look for me.

Your word arches over
the roof all day. I know it
within my bowed head, where
the other sky listens.
You will bring me
everything when the time comes.

One Night

A voice within my shadow wakened me,
a glowing voice: "I love the dark
too much—I cannot sleep." And there came
for me again one long away,
her face as it shone in candlelight.

That voice was always kind; it helped
me now to rest, in its long shadow:
"So much we loved the dark," it said,
"that all these years apart I have been
here, like this, hidden in your shade."

Third Street

They are watching me die. Six years old
and I'm dying. "Dip-theria," they call it, and my throat
won't open, and the doctor with a look at my mother
shaking his head, then the long needle stabbing
my back, my dog Buster whining, Peggy
holding her doll and crying. Shadows lengthen
and reach up the wall. They jump. They are watching me die.

Now in the strange room of my head my shadow
escapes and floats away, leaving our street
and the vinegar factory, on past the Santa Fe tracks
and fluttery lights, over the diminishing river.
How sad that Buster on his little rug will sleep
alone, that Peggy's doll will stare button eyes
all night at my pillow, my empty bed.

If only my father could hold me forever, and the world
stay still—my little blue shirt, my elkhide shoes
waiting for Buster and me to explore Alaska
and all those ranges. . . . I see our clean walls, and the sparrow
I killed with my slingshot (how it held out its wings and fell
trembling into the dust). I will live. The doctor's

black bag will save me. His long needle will stab
again into my back and Buster will howl.

My father's eyes—I see them yearn me toward him
and carry me drifting and weak to my bed in the room.
Years later my son will die and that look
will return. Something will break in the sky that was welded
and forged back home by a thousand pledges of truth.
Third Street, I hold you here, and my throat will open.

How the Real Bible Is Written

Once we painted our house and went into it.
Today, after years, I remember that color
under the new paint now old.
I look out of the windows dangerously
and begin to know more. Now when I
walk through this town there are
too many turns before the turn
I need. Listen, birds and cicadas
still trying to tell me surface things:
I have learned how the paint goes on,
and then other things—how the real Bible is
written, downward through the pages,
carved, hacked, and molded, like the faces
of saints or the planks ripped aside
by steady centuries of weather, deeper than
dust, under the moles, caught by the
inspiration in an old badger's shoulder
that bores for grizzled secrets in the ground.

Easter Morning

Maybe someone comes to the door and says,
"Repent," and you say, "Come on in," and it's
Jesus. That's when all you ever did, or said,
or even thought, suddenly wakes up again and
sings out, "I'm still here," and you know it's true.
You just shiver alive and are left standing
there suddenly brought to account: saved.

Except, maybe that someone says, "I've got a deal
for you." And you listen, because that's how
you're trained—they told you, "Always hear both sides."
So then the slick voice can sell you anything, even
Hell, which is what you're getting by listening.
Well, what should you do? I'd say always go to
the door, yes, but keep the screen locked. Then,
while you hold the Bible in one hand, lean forward
and say carefully, "Jesus?"

Fixers

On back roads you can find people
who keep machinery alive. With a file,
a wrench, a hammer they scrape, twist
and pound until the old tractor wakes up
or the plough bites again into the ground.

I've bullied rusty iron and made it
remember what to do, and once on a back road
I put out a fire under the hood of a car;
but these greasy geniuses have to conjure
miracles day after day just to keep going.

Often their audience is a customer eager to
get started again, or maybe their little daughter
watching how Daddy fixes things. And sometimes
only an old dog—wise in when to jump aside—
studies mechanics and barks when The Master says,

"There!"

You and Art

Your exact errors make a music
that nobody hears.
Your straying feet find the great dance,
walking alone.
And you live on a world where stumbling
always leads home.

Year after year fits over your face—
when there was youth, your talent
was youth;
later, you find your way by touch
where moss redeems the stone;

And you discover where music begins
before it makes any sound,
far in the mountains where canyons go
still as the always-falling, ever-new flakes of snow.

Walking the Borders

Sometimes in the evening a translator walks out
and listens by streams that wander back and forth
across borders. The translator holds a mint
on the tongue, turns it over to try
a new side, then tastes a wild new flavor,
a flavor that enlivens those fading languages
of cursing and calling each other those names
that destroyed millions by swinging a cross
like an ax, or a crescent curved like a knife,
or a star so red it burned its way over the ground.

The wild new flavor fades away too,
but lingers awhile along borders for a translator to savor
secretly, borrowing from both sides, holding
for a moment the smooth round world
in that cool instant of evening before the sun goes down.

Something That Happens Right Now

I haven't told this before. By our house on the plains before I was born my father planted a maple. At night after bedtime when others were asleep I would go out and stand beside it and know all the way north and all the way south. Air from the fields wandered in. Stars waited with me. All of us ached with a silence, needing the next thing, but quiet. We leaned into midnight and then leaned back. On the rise to the west the radio tower blinked—so many messages pouring by.

A great surge came rushing from everywhere and wrapped all the land and sky. Where were we going? How soon would our house break loose and become a little speck lost in the vast night? My father and mother would die. The maple tree would stand right there. With my hand on that smooth bark we would watch it all. Then my feet would come loose from Earth and rise by the power of longing. I wouldn't let the others know about this, but I would be everywhere, as I am right now, a thin tone like the wind, a sip of blue light—no source, no end, no horizon.

Clash

The butcher knife was there
on the table my father made.
The hatchet was on the stair;
I knew where it was.

Hot wires burned in the wall,
all the nails pointed in.
At the sound of my mother's call
I knew it was the time.

When she threatened I hid in the yard.
Policemen would come for me.
It was dark; waiting was hard.
There was something I had to win.

After my mother wept
I forgot where the hatchet was:

there was a truce we kept—
we both chose real things.

If she taunted, I grew still.
If she faltered, I lowered the knife.
I did not have to kill.
Time had made me stronger.

I won before too late,
and—adult before she died—
I had traveled from love to hate,
and partway back again.

Now all I have, my life,
—strange—comes partly from this:
I thought about a knife
when I learned that great word—"Choose."

Learning

A piccolo played, then a drum.
Feet began to come—a part
of the music. Here came a horse,
clippety clop, away.

My mother said, "Don't run—
the army is after someone
other than us. If you stay
you'll learn our enemy."

Then he came, the speaker. He stood
in the square. He told us who
to hate. I watched my mother's face,
its quiet. "That's him," she said.

Entering History

Remember the line in the sand?
You were there, on the telly, part of
the military. You didn't want to
give it but they took your money
for those lethal tanks and the bombs.

Minorities, they don't have a country
even if they vote: "Thanks, anyway,"
the majority says, and you are left there
staring at the sand and the line they drew,
calling it a challenge, calling it "ours."

Where was your money when the tanks
grumbled past? Which bombs did you buy
for the death rain that fell? Which year's
taxes put that fire to the town
where the screaming began?

Not in the Headlines

It's not the kind of thing that ought to happen; so
I'm not going to tell you about it. You wouldn't be
happy about the world, and you couldn't change anything
after all this time anyway. The girl herself moved
away, and the guys—Raymond, Oscar and Fred, all
friends of mine before it happened—they went on and
became a banker, a war hero, and a lawyer. You couldn't
tell them from other people just like them. That was the thing.

But what happened—not at the time, but after—
was that the girl's guardians didn't complain, and the girl,
being retarded a little and not knowing enough anyway,
she just went on, maybe even feeling OK, and possibly—
this is the awful part—maybe even liking it.

Where the guardians lived, and where it all happened,
was a big house on Main Street back in some trees.
I was there; so at night it comes back, the tree shadows,

the bright rooms and the party in the downstairs with
the foster parents gone and Fred turning up the Victrola.
They got around in a circle, sort of leaving me out as
usual, being a Momma's boy but partly tolerated and not
even knowing if I wanted to belong to the group, their
church, their neighborhood, their country club.

Later when people found out, the guys knew it must
have been me, the Momma's boy. Have you thought about
the role of being the one who holds back and then tells?
It all helped me know my place, a dissenter, a doubter
of all commitments to party, gang, nation, never a hero,
and then later on their war—not for me.

When I pass through that town these days, covering my
territory for whatever company it is at the time, I
read about Oscar and Fred and Raymond, their success
and their children, their wives. The girl, I don't know,
and where or anything. And why did I tell you even this
much? It won't as I say help you guide your actions
or become a banker or a war hero or a good citizen,
and it sure won't help you know how to like the world.

One Evening

On a frozen pond a mile north of Liberal
almost sixty years ago I skated wild circles
while a strange pale sun went down.

A scattering of dry brown reeds cluttered
the ice at one end of the pond, and a fitful
breeze ghosted little surface eddies of snow.

No house was in sight, no tree, only
the arched wide surface of the earth
holding the pond and me under the sky.

I would go home, confront all my years, the tangled
events to come, and never know more than I did
that evening waving my arms in the lemon-colored light.

Right to Die

God takes care of it for
everyone, once. And armies
figure it out, wholesale,
for others, in the air, on the ground,
at sea.

Living, though, is a habit
hard to shake, and they don't
move the heavy stuff at you
till later when you are about ready,
usually, any time.

Still, maybe I'd help,
knowing what I do about need and
the grim alternatives; maybe
I'd be very kind when the hurt eyes
turn, suddenly loud, toward me.

Toward the End

> *Let mine eyes see thee,*
> *sweet Jesus of Nazareth;*
> *let mine eyes see thee*
> *and then see death.*
> THERESA OF AVILA

They will give you a paperweight
carved out of heavy wood with black letters
that say everyone likes you and will miss
so steady and loyal a worker.

You carry it home and look at the nice message.
Not always have people allowed you even
a quiet exit—catcalls from that woman
who once appeared kind, plenty of lectures.

And oh the years of hovering anger
all around when each day reluctantly
opened and then followed like some dedicated,
stealthy, calculating, teasing assassin.

Now you can walk into the evening.
Walls where people live lean
on each side. You feel your mother by you
again, and your father has taken your hand.

Sister Peg skips ahead and looks back
that way we all loved and said, "Ours—
how eager she is! Beautiful!" We didn't
stay true, Peg. We didn't, we didn't.

The road bends gradually, then aims
straight at sunset. People are streaming
where all the sky opens on a bluff
and the sea drops off, blue and bright.

Suddenly this moment is worth all the rest.
Never has the sweetness arched so near
and overwhelming. They say a green flash
comes if you are lucky right at the end.

Now you see it was always there.

Whispered in Winter

Snow falls. The fields begin again
their forgiveness. All that dirt forgiven.
All along the street forgiven—the magenta
house, proud maples, the corner where
Ellen lived, a glimpse of old Barney.

Some people don't have any past.

On school mornings forgive the fog, all that
avoidance when Ruth wanted to talk,

the teacher who ridiculed mistakes,
the boy who called out "Bitch! Hellraker!"
through his fence as you walked by.

You can learn from anything.

But for some there isn't enough snow,
ever—the nails fused in a cross
they saved when the church burned,
the cemetery more silent every day.
We need a softer snow, again, again.

Again.

Old Glory

No flag touched ours this year.
Our flag ate theirs. Ours cried,
"Banner, banner," all over the sky—
the sky now ours, the sea this year
our pond. "Thus far," we said,
 "no farther," and the storm advanced,
or stopped, or hovered, depending.

We won, they say. They say good came:
we live in the shadow of our flag.
We fear no evil. Salute, ye people.
That feeling you have, they call it glory.
We own it now, they say, under God,
in the sky, on earth, as it is in Heaven.

Explaining the Big One

Remember that leader with the funny mustache?—
liked flags and marching?—gave loyalty
a bad name? Didn't drink, they say,
but liked music, and was jolly, sometimes.

And then the one with the big mustache
and the wrinkled uniform, always jovial
for the camera but eliminated malcontents
by the millions. He was our friend, I think.

Women? Oh yes, women. They danced
and sang for the soldiers or volunteered
their help. We loved them, except Tokyo
Rose—didn't we kill her, afterward?

Our own leaders?—the jaunty cigarette holder,
the one with the cigar. . . . Remember the pearl-handled
revolvers? And Ike, who played golf. It was us
against the bad guys, then. You should have been there.

At the Grave of My Brother: Bomber Pilot

Tantalized by wind, this flag that flies
to mark your grave discourages those nearby
graves, and all still marching this hillside chanting,
    "Heroes, thanks. Goodby."

If a visitor may quiz a marble sentiment,
was this tombstone quarried in that country
where you slew thousands likewise honored
    of the enemy?

Reluctant hero, drafted again each Fourth
of July, I'll bow and remember you. Who
shall we follow next? Who shall we kill
    next time?

A Memorial: Son Bret

In the way you went you were important.
I do not know what you found.
In the pattern of my life you stand
where you stood always, in the center,
a hero, a puzzle, a man.

What you might have told me
I will never know—the lips went still,
the body cold. I am afraid
in the circling stars, in the dark,
and even at noon in the light.

When I run what am I running from?
You turned once to tell me something,
but then you glimpsed a shadow on my face
and maybe thought, Why tell what hurts?
You carried it, my boy, so brave, so far.

Now we have all the days, and the sun
goes by the same; there is a faint,
wandering trail I find sometimes, off
through grass and sage. I stop
and listen: only summer again—remember?—

The bees, the wind.

Annals of *Tai Chi*: "Push Hands"

In this long routine "Push Hands,"
one recognizes force and yields, then
slides, again, again, endlessly like water,
what goes away, what follows, aggressive
courtesy till force must always lose,
lost in the seethe and retreat of ocean.

So does the sail fill, and air come
just so, because of what's gone, "Yes"

in all things, "Yes, come in if you
insist," and thus conducted find a way
out, *yin* following and becoming
by a beautiful absence its partner *yang*.

Sure You Do

Remember the person you thought you were? That summer
sleepwalking into your teens? And your body ambushing
the self that skipped from school? And you wandered into
this carnival where all the animals in the ark began
to pace and howl? The swing they strapped you in?
The descent through air that came alive, till
the pause at the top? The door on the way down
that opened on joy? And then, and then, it was
a trap. You would get used to it: like the others
you could shoulder your way through the years, take on
what came and stare without flinching, but you knew at the time
it was goodby to everything else in your life.
The great door that opened on terror swung open.

The Magic Mountain

A book opens. People come out, bend
this way and talk, ponder, love, wander around
while pages turn. Where did the plot go?
Why did someone sing just as the train
went by? Here come chapters with landscape all over
whatever happens when people meet. Now
a quiet part: a hospital glows in the dark.
I don't think that woman with the sad gray eyes
will ever come back. And what does it mean when
the Italian has so many ideas? Maybe
a war is coming. The book is ending. Everyone
has a little tremolo in them; all
are going to die and it's cold and the snow, and the clear
air. They took someone away. It's ending,
the book is ending. But I thought—never mind. It closes.

For a Daughter Gone Away

1

When they shook the box, and poured out its chances,
you were appointed to be happy. Even in a prison
they would give you the good cell, one with warm pipes
through it. And one big dream arched over everything:
it was a play after that, and your voice found its range.
What happened reached back all the time, and "the octo,"
"the isped," and other patterns with songs in them
came to you. Once on the Yukon you found a rock
shaped like a face, and better than keeping it, you placed
it carefully looking away, so that in the morning when
it woke up you were gone.

2

You saw the neighborhood, its trees growing and houses
being, and streets lying there to be run on;
you saved up afternoons, voluptuous warm old fenders
of Cadillacs in the sun, and then the turn of your thought
northward—blends of gold on scenes by Peace River. . . .

3

It was always a show, life was—dress, manners—
and always time to walk slowly: here are the rich
who view with alarm and wonder about the world
that used to be tame (they wear good clothes, be courteous);
there are the poets and critics holding their notebooks
ready for ridicule or for the note expressing
amusement (they're not for real, they perform; if you
take offense they can say, "I was just making
some art"); and here are the perceivers of injustice; they
never have to change expression; here are the officials,
the police, the military, all trying to dissemble
their sense of the power of their uniforms. (And here
at the end is a mirror—to complete the show for ourselves.)

4

Now, running alone in winter before dawn has come
I have heard from the trees a trilling sound, an owl I

suppose, a soft, hesitant voice, a woodwind, a breathy
note. Then it is quiet again, all the way out
in that space that goes on to the end of the world. And I think
of beings more lonely than we are, clinging to branches or drifting
wherever the air moves them through the dark and cold.
I make a sound back, those times, always trying for only
my place, one moving voice touching whatever is present
or might be, even what I cannot see when it comes.

Living Statues

By the rules you stop in that pose
fixed when the signal came. You scan
their faces. Your hand flung loose
almost touches Anita's hand.

If it's ever over and they don't move,
the sun floats away or the moon
sets in the tired branches of the elm.
Down the street porchlights bloom.

Rivers flow, now and then a building
crumbles, a season passes, old friends
collapse and sink into nothing.
Maybe some games never end.

There was always going to be
a better bundle of rules, a scaffolding—
a truth—beyond the houses. Breathing
the hard air you stand faithful.

Put These in Your Pipe

In a crash my head hit the pavement—
I've had the world in me ever since.

The doctor listens to my heart—
yes, I know what time it is.

I walk out and stand in a clearing
while the snow falls all around.

Children, that country you cry about,
that's where we all have to live.

Whenever the worst times came
doves have shared my sorrow.

Wherever God has sent me,
the meadowlarks were already there.

I think of something to end with,
but I'm not going to write it down.

Meditation in the Waiting Room

I have this dream, doctor: I'm living in this town
where I have become old. Neighbors too have become
old, and they stay in their houses, getting up late
and coming out only for their morning paper. Our
trees have grown thickly around us, and the hedges
reach high between. Our street stretches away, very
quiet. Is this dream all right, doctor? Is there
anything wrong with me? Sometimes everything seems
normal, but other times I feel some slow, faint
alarm come over me. This isn't the way the world

felt before. It has become much less important;
I think some good spirit or god has gone away
and left us on this aimless planet getting fainter
and quieter and smaller, spinning through the sky.

Tell me, doctor, is my dream all right to have?

Choosing a Dog

"It's love," they say. You touch
the right one and a whole half of the universe
wakes up, a new half.

Some people never find
that half, or they neglect it or trade it
for money or success and it dies.

The faces of big dogs tell, over the years,
that size is a burden: you enjoy it for awhile
but then maintenance gets to you.

When I get old I think I'll keep, not a little
dog, but a serious dog,
for the casual, drop-in criminal—

My kind of dog, unimpressed by
dress or manner, just knowing
what's really there by the smell.

Your good dogs, some things that they hear
they don't really want you to know—
it's too grim or ethereal.

And sometimes when they look in the fire
they see time going on and someone alone,
but they don't say anything.

Identities

If a life could own another life—
a wolf a deer, a fish a bird,
a man a tree—who would
exchange a life with me?

Dark in the forest a path
goes down; soft as moss
a voice comes on: my hand
on bark, my stilled face alone—

Then water, then gravel, then stone.

Assuming Control

1
Sometimes I breathe and
the time called Now intrudes.
Marching down some street, people
hand me a flag and watch
how hard I wave it.
Don't they know that in the sky
someone keeps track of the world?
Someone like Mohammed? Someone like Jesus?

2
My friends outline my weakness—inattention,
a selfish life, dull reactions.
My mouth says, "Oh." My hands
wander over my vest or vaguely follow
an invisible butterfly before me.
My face makes adjustments, but
none decisive, the mouth not quite
smiling, the eyes turning aside.

3
Have you noticed?—I notice
that people observe how stupid
I am, how obsolete my views and practices,
and my whole generation, how we enjoy
superficial styles, arts, manners.
I listen to these discoveries. I read
about my weakness. How could I
have missed the obvious truth so long?
Generously, my critics lift examples:
"There!" "And look at this." I see it;
they have a point. But it's hard to give up
what used to please me. Maybe in time I can.

4
Sometimes I breathe and
the stars go by in their serene beatitudes,
never disturbing a weather-gray house
by the sea where I have hidden my life.
My gypsy attention continues its years-long
wandering. It will return. It will find
my mouth saying, "Oh," as the ocean
rises and falls, responding
to those deliberate events in the sky—
the sun, the moon, the stars.

A Few Snorts from a Wild One

Life sleeps in this tired old horse, but might
wake yet for a spur or a fire when the muscles
come alive, till even the main gate creaks
as a shoulder hits it and makes the whole corral
shudder its rails while the weakest post
almost gives way. Some time it will, maybe
tomorrow, and then you'll see: I guarantee you
the road out of here will be filled with a horse.

There's a Thread You Follow (Poems written in 1993)

5 JANUARY 1993

The Last Class

They crowd near. If you look at them
they look down. Pause. They shuffle their feet.
Over near the windows along one side
patches of light shine on the floor.
It is almost the hour to begin
whatever comes after this day.

Over their heads you see so many
clouds and stars and days. A hook
begins to come down from the sky.
If you call out, if you warn them,
what good will that do? It is the long
moment that always opens at such times.

Now the eyes turn away. A new
high-pitched hum has compelled the others
to look around. What happens next?
You look toward the exit; this isn't
your place any more. It was coming;
now it is here, the call. Not for them—

For you. It is for you.

9 JANUARY

Putting the Sonnet to Work

Pack your heavy suitcase
when it is time to travel.
No use making the trip
just to spin the wheels.

Load that box you always
intended to deliver;
crowd in all the knickknacks
nobody ever uses.

This train carries freight.
It's on time if it gets there.
Crossroads don't count, or bells.
There's a map and a dot and an engine.

It's cargo we want—cargo:
just words won't get you there.

10 JANUARY

Charades

Willows in the wind act out "afraid."
Rocks make the sound for "nothing."
Both of those I am as a person.

My father served for the concept "Gone."
My mother was perfect for "Whine."
And their son, that's me, "Defiant."

Willow, rock, mother, father,
behold what you made: "Maybe."

11 JANUARY

Cro-Magnon
(With a phrase from Saint Theresa)

Catch and let go, leaves take sunlight.
Wind pounces on them. Deep in shadows where winter
hides lurks the ice. People slip by,
flickering feet, little darting eyes.

How soon will these natives build
cities, burn up the forest, civilize
paradise? God will sip them
like little drops of dew when it is time.

13 JANUARY

Notes for the Program

Just the ordinary days, please.
I wouldn't want them any better.

About the pace of life, it seems best to have
slow, if-I-can-stand-them revelations.

And take this message about the inevitable:
I've decided it's all right if it comes.

13 JANUARY

Style

Mary June's brother Willard always had
just a certain corner of his handkerchief
hanging out of his hip pocket. That was
my first intimation of a personal style.

My hair wouldn't comb down; so
every night for years I wore
one of Aunt Klara's silk stockings
pulled firmly on top of my head.

When we had company my mother was always
afraid I would swing my soup spoon
toward me rather than away. And I was to
leave a little, not scrape like a dog at the last.

These glimpses of decorum in my early life
have fitted me for success. My manners,
my neat handkerchief, and my tame haircut
have seen me through everyday encounters with society.

19 JANUARY

Evidence

First, this face—history did it,
winters, two world wars, long
days bent in the fields in the sun,
a few blows, fear, sorrow.

This face is evidence left over
when those years denied what happened
and stole away, the shell still whispering
of treasure and wreckage in the sea.

And then beyond this mask—that's where
everything else begins to wake up:
what the wars were about, how the field boss
discovered a truth God had in mind.

There's a bell somewhere. This face
looks up, the way old people listen.

20 JANUARY

Retirement

After that knifeblade, we breathed
a film on it like a mirror and looked up—
our children were gone, and in their place
a vacant road continued into a storm.
That's when I think we began to know
how the rest would be, the soft
careful sound of little worlds falling.

Those flakes, every one, hit
the windshield with a glad sacrifice
and then never existed. You could
look back and imagine a lifetime
of snowflake incidents again, but
this time—you could hope—with religion,
or some kind of thicker coat on.

For certain young readers:
You don't have to understand this.
Pretend that you don't understand.
Go back to your inhale-exhale
existence. Don't look up now.
There will be time.

28 JANUARY

Inscribed on a Prayer Wheel and Spun

Days bury days, then weeks, months, years,
and centuries; then on, odd on even,
even on odd, a pile, a hill, a mountain,
infinitude and start again: this world.

Time rolls on, but the axle
stays: in a story they charmed the world and it stopped,
but a fish moved through the still water. That
fish is thought. It won't rest. It won't. It won't.

In my former life in my dreams it was always dark
but something kept me warm. It folded around
and wrapped me against the cold. What was it?
In my dream I woke—it was my father's coat.

Now, awake, I build another dream:
in the big chair with leather, with brass buttons,
my father rocks again. "We lived in the snow,"
he says, "we are Indian, Asian, African."

In this, the water of Now, we swim. Our path
closes in crystal behind us; ahead it glistens.
Listen: nobody knows any more than ever.
My father rocks; the brass buttons are shining.

2 FEBRUARY

Writing It Down

We pitied our uncle, the odd face
he wore. He couldn't help being
a philosopher. When we danced
his feet didn't know how to lead—
or even how to follow.

Aunt Sarah found the right place for her,
a hidden room with a secret door.
She couldn't get out, when the time came.

Father just went on, the only way
he knew. His head bent lower
and his eyes pierced far. At the last
he shuffled and all the light was gone.

In my book I fold these things I saw
and a few other things that shadows
brought around, like how to lift
your dreams when seabirds are crying,
or when the fog is in how to find the sun.

I leave, Mother, you for others
to carry. We are alike and the world
imprisoned us. All my life I've
tapped out our kind of truth.

For nine months I studied what
your heart was saying.

15 FEBRUARY

Mein Kampf

In those reaches of the night when your thoughts
burrow in, or at some stabbed interval
pinned by a recollection in daylight,
a better self begs its hands out to you:

That bitter tracery your life wove
looms forth, and the jagged times haggle
and excruciate your reaching palms again—
"A dull knife hurts most."

Old mistakes come calling: no life
happens just once. Whatever snags
even the edge of your days will abide.
You are a turtle with all the years on your back.

Your head sinks down into the mud.
You must bear it. You need a thick shell in that rain.

15 FEBRUARY

Things That Hurt Me—

Turn into pearls.
First my tongue turns them over and over.
They have an edge that lacerates
    and then brings out a coating.
They begin to shine.

I can't leave them alone. They take on
   that lustre of suffering made pure.
They accumulate as decorations around my neck
   or dangle from my ears.
Trophies have a polish. You hold them close.
   But they hide a hollow of pain.

18 FEBRUARY

Sayings of the Blind

Feeling is believing.

Mountains don't exist. But their slopes do.

Little people have low voices.

All things, even the rocks, make a little noise.

The silence back of all sound is called "the sky."

There's a big stranger in town called the sun.
   He doesn't speak to us but puts out a hand.

Night opens a door into a cellar—
   you can smell it coming.

On Sundays everyone stands farther apart.

Velvet feels black.

Meeting cement is never easy.

What do they mean when they say night is gloomy?

Edison didn't invent much.

Whenever you wake up it's morning.

Names have a flavor.

17 MARCH

Real People

Trees are afraid of storms. Even oaks
will do anything when the wind blows—
they'll bow, they'll spend their leaves.

In the tropics, imprisoned by vines, one race of giants
has stood around for centuries teased by monkeys
and snakes. Hearts down there have grown hard
as iron, and limbs have writhed out a jungle story.

A whole forest in Siberia fell at the knees of
an unknown emperor so terrible no one ever
said his name, and those trees never got up again.

If you go hiking up in the mountains
you find miles of stumps where trees have
run away, panicked by the sound of a saw.

There is one tribe that has trudged far north
to wait with little round shoulders for the cruel snow.
Sometimes one raven wings by asking where justice is.
And low along streams there—the abject willows.
They're poor. But they never ask for anything.

25 MARCH

Just Thinking

Got up on a cool morning. Leaned out a window.
No cloud, no wind. Air that flowers held
for awhile. Some dove somewhere.

Been on probation most of my life. And
the rest of my life been condemned. So these moments
count for a lot—peace, you know.

Let the bucket of memory down into the well,
bring it up. Cool, cool minutes. No one
stirring, no plans. Just being there.

This is what the whole thing is about.

1 APRIL

No Praise, No Blame

What have the clouds been up to today? You can't
blame them, you know. Their edges just
happen, and where they go is the fault of the wind.
I'd like my arrival to be like that, alone and
quiet, really present but never to blame.

And I'd never presume or apologize, and if anyone
pressed me I'd be gone, and come back there
only some harmless, irresistible presence
all around you, like the truth, something you need,
like the air.

16 APRIL

Afterwards

Mostly you look back and say, "Well, OK. Things might have
been different, sure, and it's too bad, but look—
things happen like that, and you did what you could."
You go back and pick up the pieces. There's tomorrow.
There's that long bend in the river on the way
home. Fluffy bursts of milkweed are floating
through shafts of sunlight or disappearing where
trees reach out from their deep dark roots.

Maybe people have to go in and out of shadows
till they learn that floating, that immensity

waiting to receive whatever arrives with trust.
Maybe somebody has to explore what happens
when one of us wanders over near the edge
and falls for awhile. Maybe it was your turn.

22 APRIL

Where We Are

Fog in the morning here
will make some of the world far away
and the near only a hint. But rain
will feel its blind progress along the valley,
tapping to convert one boulder at a time
into a glistening fact. Daylight will love what came.
Whatever fits will be welcome, whatever
steps back in the fog will disappear
and hardly exist. You hear the river
saying a prayer for all that's gone.

Far over the valley there is an island
for everything left; and our own island
will drift there too, unless we hold on,
unless we tap like this: "Friend,
are you there? Will you touch when
you pass, like the rain?"

7 MAY

Slow News from Our Place

It isn't that the blossoms fall, Ezra.
It isn't that certain vagueness, Wallace.
It isn't even how those flies buzz,
either, Emily. It's only the plains
out here, how they take it all and wait,

morning, evening, night, forever;
how they don't move, no matter what
Galileo says, or The Church, or God himself.

We stand on the ground, out here. Go ahead, speakers;
tell us your theories, your judgments, the latest assessments
from the centers of power, any styles or truths you like.
We're out by The Platte, The Missouri,
The Smoky Hill. We're quiet on this slow scanner
The Earth, under its arch of sky.
Go ahead. Tell us. We're listening.

17 MAY

Emily, This Place, and You

She got out of the car here one day,
and it was snowing a little. She could see
little glimpses of those mountains, and away down
there by the river the curtain of snow would
shift, and those deep secret places looked
all the more mysterious. It was quiet, you know.

Her life seemed quiet, too. There had been troubles,
sure—everyone has some. But now, looking out there,
she felt easy, at home in the world—maybe like
a casual snowflake. And some people loved her.
She would remember that. And remember this place.

As you will, wherever you go after this day,
just a stop by the road, and a glimpse of someone's life,
and your own, too, how you can look out any time,
just being part of things, getting used to being a person,
taking it easy, you know.

24 MAY

Quo Vadis

Sometimes I choose a cloud and let it
cross the sky floating me away.
Or a bird unravels its song and carries me
as it flies deeper and deeper into the woods.

Is there a way to be gone and still
belong? Travel that takes you home?

Is that life?—to stand by a river and go.

2 JUNE

"It's heavy to drag, this big sack . . ."

It's heavy to drag, this big sack of what
you should have done. And finally
you can't lift it any more.
Someone says, "Come on," and you
just look at them. Trees are waiting,
mountains. You never intended
that it should come to this.

But Now has arrived and is looking
straight at you, the way a lion does
when thinking it over, and anything
can happen. It's time for the cavalry
or maybe the Lone Ranger. But they
won't come. Maybe the music will
spill over and start it all again.
Maybe.

14 JUNE

Crossing Our Campground

Part of the time when I move it's for
Bret. On the path my feet nimble along,
avoiding a root, adjusting easily to some
rough place and lightly stepping on.

This is for you, Bret, I think; this
is the way an old man walks who still
stays vigorous and strong, firm, alert,
holding on through the years for you—

The kind of old man you could be,
    or could have been.

16 JUNE

Godiva County, Montana

She's a big country. Her undulations
roll and flow in the sun. Those flanks
quiver when the wind caresses the grass.
Who turns away when so generous a body
offers to play hide-and-seek all summer?
One shoulder leans bare all the way up
the mountain; limbs range and plunge
wildly into the river. We risk our eyes
every day; they celebrate; they dance
and flirt over this offered treasure.
"Be alive," the land says. "Listen—
this is your time, your world, your pleasure."

17 JUNE

Jeremiah at Miminagish

Somewhere up there God has poised
the big answer to the new doctrine
written all over this country in concrete
by the corporation everyone has bought into
that leads to where the minotaur waits,

Waits just over there by the new mall,
or at the end of your carefully planned
university course, your Moloch Award,
your honors, your degree fastened like
a dogtag around your neck for life,

As the freeways are knotting around cities
getting ready to reach out.
But scattered in little pieces the old times
trail off into the mountains and hide,
forming their avalanche. Then salvation.

13 JULY

Hunger

When it's your own pain, you notice it.
A bird that sings when you go by.
No road goes far enough—you understand?
And no sound can find the note—some call
has caught what wrings hope out of
evil history. But we can't reach it,
hear it, find a way to deserve even
the immediate offering. I reach far beyond
the music, run forth to contemplate
a clod, or a mountain. They help, yes,
but no road goes far enough. You understand?

19–21 JULY

Ways to Live

1. India

In India in their lives they happen
again and again, being people or
animals. And if you live well
your next time could be even better.

That's why they often look into your eyes
and you know some far-off story
with them and you in it, and some
animal waiting over at the side.

Who would want to happen just once?
It's too abrupt that way, and
when you're wrong, it's too late
to go back—you've done it forever.

And you can't have that soft look when you
pass, the way they do it in India.

2. Having It Be Tomorrow

Day, holding its lantern before it,
moves over the whole earth slowly
to brighten that edge and push it westward.
Shepherds on upland pastures begin fires
for breakfast, beads of light that extend
miles of horizon. Then it's noon and
coasting toward a new tomorrow.

If you're in on that secret, a new land
will come every time the sun goes
climbing over it, and the welcome of children
will remain every day new in your heart.
Those around you don't have it new,
and they shake their heads turning gray every
morning when the sun comes up. And you laugh.

3. Being Nice and Old

After their jobs are done old people
cackle together. They look back and shiver,
all of that was so dizzying when it happened;
and now if there is any light at all it
knows how to rest on the faces of friends.
And any people you don't like, you just turn
the page a little more and wait while they
find out what time is and begin to bend
lower; or you can just turn away and
let them drop off the edge of the world.

4. Good Ways to Live

At night outside it all moves or
almost moves—trees, grass,
touches of wind. The room you have
in the world is ready to change.
Clouds parade by, and stars in their
configurations. Birds from far
touch the fabric around them—you can
feel their wings move. Somewhere under
the earth it waits, that emanation
of all things. It breathes. It pulls you
slowly out through doors or windows
and you spread in the thin halo of night mist.

28 JULY

Living on the Plains [1993]

Carefully, sending leaves always toward the sun,
a vine climbs its trellis—even today
honeysuckle means Dakota and long summer afternoons.

We lived by what the river did, and how
seasons curve into and away from each other,
leaning into your face and peering hard.

If you come back years later your name
will be there carved on the windowsill
in the hayloft, under the dust.

Time doesn't hurry any more the way
it did along about school bell or when
the clock heard night outside and the snow falling.

If you ever climb the map again
you could stop there and whisper a few hymns,
the ones that civilized Dodge, Cody, Abilene.

30 JULY

Our Way Those Days before These Days

Today a kind of sound shadow lulls along the street,
the quell of an August afternoon. Whatever
the earth intends, whatever hovers around
our town, waits for a signal from September.
And sometime if tomorrow comes maybe a bird
will call through the woods again and it will be
autumn, with blue and clouds, a breeze from the ocean
where dreamers go forth looking for selfhood.

When we scattered along through the forest eating
and chattering, often we'd stop in a clearing
where sunlight poured through, and we'd sing
for awhile before going on. One would
begin with a tune till the rest couldn't help it—
they'd have to join, often beating on a log
or stamping their feet on the ground in unison.

Often away off other groups would hear.
We'd know by their faint sounds imitating
ours. There were times when the wind
would carry that music while branches waved
high in the trees. Birds would join in
while our young ones danced back and forth,
Heaven there in the woods those days.

1 AUGUST

Haycutters

Time tells them. They go along touching
the grass, the feathery ends. When it feels
just so, they start the mowing machine,
leaving the land its long windrows,
and air strokes the leaves dry.

Sometimes you begin to push; you want to
hurry the sun, have the hours expand, because
clouds come. Lightning looks out from their hearts.
You try to hope the clouds away.
"Some year we'll have perfect hay."

2 AUGUST

The Way It Is

There's a thread you follow. It goes among
things that change. But it doesn't change.
People wonder about what you are pursuing.
You have to explain about the thread.
But it is hard for others to see.
While you hold it you can't get lost.
Tragedies happen; people get hurt
or die; and you suffer and get old.
Nothing you do can stop time's unfolding.
You don't ever let go of the thread.

6 AUGUST, HIROSHIMA DAY

November

From the sky in the form of snow
comes the great forgiveness.
Rain grown soft, the flakes descend

and rest; they nestle close, each one
arrived, welcomed and then at home.

If the sky lets go some day and I'm
requested for such volunteering
toward so clean a message, I'll come.
The world goes on and while friends touch down
beside me, I too will come.

10 AUGUST

Big Bang

A shudder goes through the universe, even
long after. Every star, clasping its
meaning as it looks back, races outward
where something quiet and far waits.
Within, too, ever receding into its fractions,
that first brutal sound nestles closer
and closer toward the tiny dot of tomorrow.
And here we are in the middle, holding
it all together, not even shaking.

Hard to believe.

25 AUGUST

Joe's Corner

That is his jacket. These are
the shoes. Over there propped
where those pictures wait
you can see the staff.

Some things are heavy to carry,
so we didn't keep any more.
Those were the days, you know,
when we thought there would be tomorrows.

25 AUGUST

Home State

You can see mountains propped there,
a little bit blue. Rivers yearn through
those canyons, and storms punctuate
even the summer days.
Sometimes whole sides of the world
lean against where you live.
Just being there is a career.
And the danger is in forgetting
that sometime you might go away.

25 AUGUST

"At noon comes the lift . . ."

At noon comes the lift—sunlight
pries open a first section of afternoon
so that my shadow can begin a career.

With a little wise adjustment my whole life
might move into some phase not evident
when my parents made their plans.

Quiet as the sun, my breathing slides
past barriers and hours; "Night, I'm coming,"
my little spaceship calls.

And, oh, all else is waiting for whatever
turn my fate gives forth toward evening
and the dark and the patient stars.

26 AUGUST

You Reading This, Be Ready

Starting here, what do you want to remember?
How sunlight creeps along a shining floor?
What scent of old wood hovers, what softened
sound from outside fills the air?

Will you ever bring a better gift for the world
than the breathing respect that you carry
wherever you go right now? Are you waiting
for time to show you some better thoughts?

When you turn around, starting here, lift this
new glimpse that you found; carry into evening
all that you want from this day. This interval you spent
reading or hearing this, keep it for life—

What can anyone give you greater than now,
starting here, right in this room, when you turn around?

27 AUGUST

At Fourth and Main in Liberal, Kansas, 1932

An instant sprang at me, a winter instant,
a thin gray panel of evening. Slanted
shadows leaned from a line of trees where rain
had slicked the sidewalk. No one was there—
it was only a quick flash of a scene,
unplanned, without connection to anything
that meant more than itself, but I carried it
onward like a gift from a child who knows
that the giving is what is important, the paper, the ribbon,
the holding of breath and surprise, the friends around,
and God holding it out to you, even a rock
or a slice of evening, and behind it the whole world.

28 AUGUST

"Are you Mr. William Stafford?"

"Are you Mr. William Stafford?"
"Yes, but...."

Well, it was yesterday.
Sunlight used to follow my hand.
And that's when the strange siren-like sound flooded
over the horizon and rushed through the streets of our town.
That's when sunlight came from behind
a rock and began to follow my hand.

"It's for the best," my mother said—"Nothing can
ever be wrong for anyone truly good."
So later the sun settled back and the sound
faded and was gone. All along the streets every
house waited, white, blue, gray; trees
were still trying to arch as far as they could.

You can't tell when strange things with meaning
will happen. I'm [still] here writing it down
just the way it was. "You don't have to
prove anything," my mother said. "Just be ready
for what God sends." I listened and put my hand
out in the sun again. It was all easy.

Well, it was yesterday. And the sun came,
Why
It came.

Stories That Could Be True

FROM *Stories That Could Be True* (1977)

Our Story

Remind me again—together we
trace our strange journey, find
each other, come on laughing.
Some time we'll cross where life
ends. We'll both look back
as far as forever, that first day.
I'll touch you—a new world then.
Stars will move a different way.
We'll both end. We'll both begin.

Remind me again.

A Story That Could Be True

If you were exchanged in the cradle and
your real mother died
without ever telling the story
then no one knows your name,
and somewhere in the world
your father is lost and needs you
but you are far away.

He can never find
how true you are, how ready.
When the great wind comes
and the robberies of the rain
you stand on the corner shivering.
The people who go by—
you wonder at their calm.

They miss the whisper that runs
any day in your mind,
"Who are you really, wanderer?"—

and the answer you have to give
no matter how dark and cold
the world around you is:
"Maybe I'm a king."

Wovoka's Witness

1

The people around me,
they meet me. Often they will talk, and
listen. They give regard, and I
to them. A few can't respond. Their faces
are dead. When these people meet me
and fail, I am sorry for them. For them
it is already the end of the world.

2

You people, my eyes are taking your picture
and putting it on a ribbon that winds
inside my head. My ears capture your voice
to hold for lonely years. My hands
have a game: "Are you there? Are you there?"
Remember? We play that game
again and again.

3

My people, now it is time
for us all to shake hands with the rain.
It's a neighbor, lives here all winter.
Talkative, yes. It will tap late
at night on your door and stay there
gossiping. It goes away without a goodby
leaving its gray touch on old wood.
Where the rain's giant shoulders make a silver
robe and shake it, there are wide places.
There are cliffs where the rain leans, and
lakes that give thanks for miles

into the mountains. We owe the rain
a pat on the back—barefoot, it has walked
with us with its silver passport all over the world.

4

My own people, now listen—if we fail
all the trees in the forest will cease
to exist, or only their ghosts will stand
there fooling everyone. The wind will
pretend and the mountains will step back
through their miles of drenching fake rain.
Listen now—we must let the others make movies
of us. Be brave. Charge into their cameras
and bring them alive. They too
may dream. They too may find
the ghost dance, and be real.

Things in the Wild Need Salt

Of the many histories, Earth tells only one—
Earth misses many things people tell about,
like maybe there are earthquakes that we should have had,
or animals that know more love than God ever felt.

And we need these things: things in the wild need salt.

Once in a cave a little bar of light
fell into my hand. The walls leaned over me.
I carried it outside to let the stars look;
they peered in my hand. Stars are like that.

Do not be afraid—I no longer carry it.
But when I see a face now, splinters of that light
fall and won't go out, no matter how faint
the buried star shines back there in the cave.

It is in the earth wherever I walk.
It is in the earth wherever I walk.

Accountability

Cold nights outside the taverns in Wyoming
pickups and big semis lounge idling, letting their
haunches twitch now and then in gusts of powder snow,
their owners inside for hours, forgetting as well
as they can the miles, the circling plains, the still town
that connects to nothing but cold and space and a few
stray ribbons of pavement, icy guides to nothing
but bigger towns and other taverns that glitter and wait:
Denver, Cheyenne.

Hibernating in the library of the school on the hill
a few pieces by Thomas Aquinas or Saint Teresa
and the fragmentary explorations of people like Alfred
North Whitehead crouch and wait amid research folders
on energy and military recruitment posters glimpsed
by the hard stars. The school bus by the door, a yellow
mound, clangs open and shut as the wind finds a loose
door and worries it all night, letting the hollow
students count off and break up and blow away
over the frozen ground.

A Message from the Wanderer

Today outside your prison I stand
and rattle my walking stick: Prisoners, listen;
you have relatives outside. And there are
thousands of ways to escape.

Years ago I bent my skill to keep my
cell locked, had chains smuggled to me in pies,
and shouted my plans to jailers;
but always new plans occurred to me,
or the new heavy locks bent hinges off,
or some stupid jailer would forget
and leave the keys.

Inside, I dreamed of constellations—
those feeding creatures outlined by stars,
their skeletons a darkness between jewels,
heroes that exist only where they are not.

Thus freedom always came nibbling my thought,
just as—often, in light, on the open hills—
you can pass an antelope and not know
and look back, and then—even before you see—
there is something wrong about the grass.
And then you see.

That's the way everything in the world is waiting.

Now—these few more words, and then I'm
gone: Tell everyone just to remember
their names, and remind others, later, when we
find each other. Tell the little ones
to cry and then go to sleep, curled up
where they can. And if any of us get lost,
if any of us cannot come all the way—
remember: there will come a time when
all we have said and all we have hoped
will be all right.

There will be that form in the grass.

At the Playground

Away down deep and away up high,
a swing drops you into the sky.
Back, it draws you away down deep,
forth, it flings you in a sweep
all the way to the stars and back
—Goodby, Jill; Goodby, Jack:
shuddering climb wild and steep,
away up high, away down deep.

Artist, Come Home

Remember how bright it is,
the old rabbitbush by the hall light?

One of the blackberry vines has
reached all the way to the clothesline.

There isn't any way to keep
the kitchen window from tapping.

The tea kettle had one of its meditative
spells yesterday.

I am thinking again of that old
plan—breakfast first, then the newspaper.

They say maybe they won't have
that big war this year after all.

A frog is living under the
back step.

Wild Horse Lore

Downhill, any gait will serve.

It tastes good—a little snow
    on old hay.

A stylish mane finds
    the wind.

The world, and enough grass—
    we don't need the cavalry
    any more.

On a Church Lawn

Dandelion cavalry, light little saviors,
baffle the wind, they ride so light.
They surround a church and outside the window
utter their deaf little cry: "If you listen
well, music won't have to happen."

After service they depart singly
to mention in the world their dandelion faith:
"God is not big; He is right."

The Little Girl by the Fence at School

Grass that was moving found all shades of brown,
moved them along, flowed autumn away
galloping southward where summer had gone.

And that was the morning someone's heart stopped
and all became still. A girl said, "Forever?"
And the grass: "Yes. Forever." While the sky—

The sky—the sky—the sky.

Growing Up

One of my wings beat faster,
I couldn't help it—
the one away from the light.

It hurt to be told all the time
how I loved that terrible flame.

At the Un-National Monument along the Canadian Border

This is the field where the battle did not happen,
where the unknown soldier did not die.
This is the field where grass joined hands,
where no monument stands,
and the only heroic thing is the sky.

Birds fly here without any sound,
unfolding their wings across the open.
No people killed—or were killed—on this ground
hallowed by neglect and an air so tame
that people celebrate it by forgetting its name.

Ask Me

Some time when the river is ice ask me
mistakes I have made. Ask me whether
what I have done is my life. Others
have come in their slow way into
my thought, and some have tried to help
or to hurt: ask me what difference
their strongest love or hate has made.

I will listen to what you say.
You and I can turn and look
at the silent river and wait. We know
the current is there, hidden; and there
are comings and goings from miles away
that hold the stillness exactly before us.
What the river says, that is what I say.

A Bird inside a Box

A bird inside a box, a box will
sing. You put it in a window
for the sun—at first the song
hides, then it calls to everyone.

Every day let loose again, those
faithful notes, they're gone, they're
gone—so many deathless vows—
and songs—and friends.

Young, you tremble. Old, you do
again, in fear. Between, a rock
inside, you hold the wild bird still
like this, in here, in here.

The Moment Again

In breath, where kingdoms hide,
one little turn at the end
is king, again, again, again.
That moment hides in the breath
to be time's king: others may vaunt;
that one will never pretend.

The moment that hides in the breath
to be king when kingdoms end
waits when you dial a number:
wire hums; day blooms; light
breaks into a cave; a faint
calm voice floats forward—

You remember a screen door slam,
a scribble of sound, other days. . . .
Then the moment that hides in the breath

to be time's king moves away,
alive in its wave, never in haste,
as you say "Hello" to whoever it is,

Waiting again.

A Bridge Begins in the Trees

In an owl cry, night became real night;
from that owl cry night came
on the nerve. I felt the shock
and rolled into the dark upon my feet
listening. There was no wind.

Among the firs my fire was almost out;
I heard the lake shore tapping, then
what was no wind, a cry
within the owl cry, behind the cross
of dark the mountain made.

"Honest love will come near fire," I cried,
"and counts all partway friendship a despair."
(For that night sound had struck a nerve,
a crazybone; or some old crag had lapsed,
or just the fire had died.)

My voice went echoing, inventing response
around the world for all of our greatest need,
the longest arc, toward Friend, from All Alone.
For that brief tenure my old faith
sang again along the bone.

Peace Walk

We wondered what our walk should mean,
taking that un-march quietly;
the sun stared at our signs—"Thou shalt not kill."

Men by a tavern said, "Those foreigners. . ."
to a woman with a fur, who turned away—
like an elevator going down, their look at us.

Along a curb, their signs lined across,
a picket line stopped and stared
the whole width of the street, at ours: "Unfair."

Above our heads the sound truck blared—
by the park, under the autumn trees—
it said that love could fill the atmosphere:

Occur, slow the other fallout, unseen,
on islands everywhere—fallout, falling
unheard. We held our poster up to shade our eyes.

At the end we just walked away;
no one was there to tell us where to leave the signs.

Whispered into the Ground

Where the wind ended and we came down
it was all grass. Some of us found
a way to the dirt—easy and rich.
When it rained, we grew, except
those of us caught up in leaves, not touching
earth, which always starts things.
Often we sent off our own
just as we'd done, floating that
wonderful wind that promised new land.

Here now spread low, flat on this
precious part of the world, we miss

those dreams and the strange old places
we left behind. We quietly wait.
The wind keeps telling us something
we want to pass on to the world:
Even far things are real.

FROM *West of Your City* (1960)

Midwest

West of your city into the fern
sympathy, sympathy rolls the train
all through the night on a lateral line
where the shape of game fish tapers down
from a reach where cougar paws touch water.

Corn that the starving Indians held
all through moons of cold for seed
and then they lost in stony ground
the gods told them to plant it in—
west of your city that corn still lies.

Cocked in that land tactile as leaves
wild things wait crouched in those valleys
west of your city outside your lives
in the ultimate wind, the whole land's wave.
Come west and see; touch these leaves.

One Home

Mine was a Midwest home—you can keep your world.
Plain black hats rode the thoughts that made our code.
We sang hymns in the house; the roof was near God.

The light bulb that hung in the pantry made a wan light,
but we could read by it the names of preserves—
outside, the buffalo grass, and the wind in the night.

A wildcat sprang at Grandpa on the Fourth of July
when he was cutting plum bushes for fuel,
before Indians pulled the West over the edge of the sky.

To anyone who looked at us we said, "My friend";
liking the cut of a thought, we could say "Hello."
(But plain black hats rode the thoughts that made our code.)

The sun was over our town; it was like a blade.
Kicking cottonwood leaves we ran toward storms.
Wherever we looked the land would hold us up.

Ceremony

On the third finger of my left hand
under the bank of the Ninnescah
a muskrat whirled and bit to the bone.
The mangled hand made the water red.

That was something the ocean would remember:
I saw me in the current flowing through the land,
rolling, touching roots, the world incarnadined,
and the river richer by a kind of marriage.

While in the woods an owl started quavering
with drops like tears I raised my arm.
Under the bank a muskrat was trembling
with meaning my hand would wear forever.

In that river my blood flowed on.

In the Deep Channel

Setting a trotline after sundown
if we went far enough away in the night
sometimes up out of deep water
would come a secret-headed channel cat,

Eyes that were still eyes in the rush of darkness,
flowing feelers noncommittal and black,
and hidden in the fins those rasping bone daggers,
with one spiking upward on its back.

We would come at daylight and find the line sag,
the fishbelly gleam and the rush on the tether:
to feel the swerve and the deep current
which tugged at the tree roots below the river.

Circle of Breath

The night my father died the moon shone on the snow.
I drove in from the west; mother was at the door.
All the light in the room extended like a shadow.
Truant from knowing, I stood where the great dark fell.

There was a time before, something we used to tell—
how we parked the car in a storm and walked into a field
to know how it was to be cut off, out in the dark alone.
My father and I stood together while the storm went by.

A windmill was there in the field giving its little cry
while we stood calm in ourselves, knowing we could go home.
But I stood on the skull of the world the night he died, and knew
that I leased a place to live with my white breath.

Truant no more, I stepped forward and learned his death.

Listening

My father could hear a little animal step,
or a moth in the dark against the screen,
and every far sound called the listening out
into places where the rest of us had never been.

More spoke to him from the soft wild night
than came to our porch for us on the wind;
we would watch him look up and his face go keen
till the walls of the world flared, widened.

My father heard so much that we still stand
inviting the quiet by turning the face,
waiting for a time when something in the night
will touch us too from that other place.

A Visit Home

In my sixties I will buy a hat
and wear it as my father did.
At the corner of Central and Main.

There may be flowers by the courthouse windows
and rich offices where those town-men
cheated him in 1929.

For calculation has exploded—
boom, war, oil wells, and, God!
the slow town-men eyes and blue-serge luck.

But at the door of the library I'll lean my cane
and put my hand on buckshot
books: Dewey, Parrington, Veblen . . .

There will be many things in the slant of my hat
at the corner of Central and Main.

The Farm on the Great Plains

A telephone line goes cold;
birds tread it wherever it goes.
A farm back of a great plain
tugs an end of the line.

I call that farm every year,
ringing it, listening, still;
no one is home at the farm,
the line gives only a hum.

Some year I will ring the line
on a night at last the right one,
and with an eye tapered for braille
from the phone on the wall

I will see the tenant who waits—
the last one left at the place;
through the dark my braille eye
will lovingly touch his face.

"Hello, is Mother at home?"
No one is home today.
"But Father—he should be there."
No one—no one is here.

"But you—are you the one . . . ?"
Then the line will be gone
because both ends will be home:
no space, no birds, no farm.

My self will be the plain,
wise as winter is gray,
pure as cold posts go
pacing toward what I know.

Walking West

Anyone with quiet pace who
walks a gray road in the West
may hear a badger underground where
in deep flint another time is

Caught by flint and held forever,
the quiet pace of God stopped still.
Anyone who listens walks on
time that dogs him single file,

To mountains that are far from people,
the face of the land gone gray like flint.
Badgers dig their little lives there,
quiet-paced the land lies gaunt,

The railroad dies by a yellow depot,
town falls away toward a muddy creek.
Badger-gray the sod goes under
a river of wind, a hawk on a stick.

Our People

Under the killdeer cry
our people hunted all day
graying toward winter, their lodges
thin to the north wind's edge.

Watching miles of marsh grass
take the supreme caress,
they looked out over the earth,
and the north wind felt like the truth.

Fluttering in that wind
they stood there on the world,
clenched in their own lived story
under the killdeer cry.

In the Oregon Country

From old Fort Walla Walla and the Klickitats
to Umpqua near Port Orford, stinking fish tribes
massacred our founders, the thieving whites.

Chief Rotten Belly slew them at a feast;
Kamiakin riled the Snakes and Yakimas;
all spurted arrows through the Cascades west.

Those tribes became debris on their own lands:
Captain Jack's wide face above the rope,
his Modoc women dead with twitching hands.

The last and the most splendid, Nez Percé
Chief Joseph, fluttering eagles through Idaho,
dashed his pony-killing getaway.

They got him. Repeating rifles bored at his head,
and in one fell look Chief Joseph saw the game
out of that spiral mirror all explode.

Back of the Northwest map their country goes,
mountains yielding and hiding fold on fold,
gorged with yew trees that were good for bows.

Weather Report

Light wind at Grand Prairie, drifting snow.
Low at Vermilion, forty degrees of frost.
Lost in the Barrens, hunting over spines of ice,
the great sled dog Shadow is running for his life.

All who hear—in your wide horizon of thought
caught in this cold, the world all going gray—
pray for the frozen dead at Yellow Knife.
These words we send are becoming parts of their night.

Vacation

One scene as I bow to pour her coffee:—

> Three Indians in the scouring drouth
> huddle at a grave scooped in the gravel,
> lean to the wind as our train goes by.
> Someone is gone.
> There is dust on everything in Nevada.

I pour the cream.

At the Bomb Testing Site

At noon in the desert a panting lizard
waited for history, its elbows tense,
watching the curve of a particular road
as if something might happen.

It was looking at something farther off
than people could see, an important scene
acted in stone for little selves
at the flute end of consequences.

There was just a continent without much on it
under a sky that never cared less.
Ready for a change, the elbows waited.
The hands gripped hard on the desert.

The Fish Counter at Bonneville

Downstream they have killed the river and built a dam;
by that power they wire to here a light:
a turbine strides high poles to spit its flame
at this flume going down. A spot glows white
where an old man looks on at the ghosts of the game
in the flickering twilight—deep dumb shapes that glide.

So many Chinook souls, so many Silverside.

Watching the Jet Planes Dive

We must go back and find a trail on the ground
back of the forest and mountain on the slow land;
we must begin to circle on the intricate sod.
By such wild beginnings without help we may find
the small trail on through the buffalo-bean vines.

We must go back with noses and the palms of our hands,
and climb over the map in far places, everywhere,
and lie down whenever there is doubt and sleep there.
If roads are unconnected we must make a path,
no matter how far it is, or how lowly we arrive.

We must find something forgotten by everyone alive,
and make some fabulous gesture when the sun goes down
as they do by custom in little Mexico towns
where they crawl for some ritual up a rocky steep.
The jet planes dive; we must travel on our knees.

The Move to California

1
The Summons in Indiana

In the crept hours on our street
(repaired by snow that winter night)
from the west an angel of blown newspaper
was coming toward our house out of the dark.

Under all the far streetlights
and along all the near housefronts
silence was painting what it was given
that in that instant I was to know.

Starting up, mittened by sleep, I thought
of the sweeping stars and the wide night,
remembering as well as I could the hedges
back home that minister to comprehended fields—

And other such limits to hold the time near,
for I felt among strangers on a meteor
trying to learn their kind of numbers
to scream together in a new kind of algebra.

That night the angel went by in the dark,
but left a summons: Try farther west.
And it did no good to try to read it again:
there are things you cannot learn through manyness.

2
Glimpsed on the Way

Think of the miles we left,
and then the one slow cliff
coming across the north,
and snow.

From then on, wherever north was,
hovering over us

always it would go,
everywhere.

I wander that desert yet
whenever we draw toward night.
Somewhere ahead that cliff
still goes.

3
At the Summit

Past the middle of the continent—
wheatfields turning in God's hand
green to pale to yellow,
like the season gradual—
we approached the summit
prepared to face the imminent
map of all our vision,
the sudden look at new land.

As we stopped there, neutral,
standing on the Great Divide,
alpine flora, lodgepole pine
fluttering down on either side—
a little tree just three feet high
shared our space between the clouds,
opposing all the veering winds.
Unhurried, we went down.

4
Springs near Hagerman

Water leaps from lava near Hagerman,
piles down riverward over rock
reverberating tons of exploding shock
out of that stilled world.

We halted there once. In that cool
we drank, for back and where we had to go

lay our jobs and Idaho,
    lying far from such water.

At work when I vision that sacred land—
the vacation of mist over its rock wall—
I go blind with hope. That plumed fall
    is bright to remember.

5
Along Highway 40

Those who wear green glasses through Nevada
travel a ghastly road in unbelievable cars
and lose pale dollars
under violet hoods when they park at gambling houses.

I saw those martyrs—all sure of their cars in the open
and always believers in any handle they pulled—
wracked on an invisible cross
and staring at a green table.

While the stars were watching
I crossed the Sierras in my old Dodge
letting the speedometer measure God's kindness,
and slept in the wilderness on the hard ground.

6
Written on the Stub of the First Paycheck

Gasoline makes game scarce.
In Elko, Nevada, I remember a stuffed wildcat
someone had shot on Bing Crosby's ranch.
I stood in the filling station
breathing fumes and reading the snarl of a map.

There were peaks to the left so high
they almost got away in the heat;
Reno and Las Vegas were ahead.
I had promise of the California job,
and three kids with me.

It takes a lot of miles to equal one wildcat
today. We moved into a housing tract.
Every dodging animal carries my hope in Nevada.
It has been a long day, Bing.
Wherever I go is your ranch.

Bi-Focal

Sometimes up out of this land
a legend begins to move.
Is it a coming near
of something under love?

Love is of the earth only,
the surface, a map of roads
leading wherever go miles
or little bushes nod.

Not so the legend under,
fixed, inexorable,
deep as the darkest mine
the thick rocks won't tell.

As fire burns the leaf
and out of the green appears
the vein in the center line
and the legend veins under there,

So, the world happens twice—
once what we see it as;
second it legends itself
deep, the way it is.

Outside

The least little sound sets the coyotes walking,
walking the edge of our comfortable earth.
We look inward, but all of them
are looking toward us as they walk the earth.

We need to let animals loose in our houses,
the wolf to escape with a pan in his teeth,
and streams of animals toward the horizon
racing with something silent in each mouth.

For all we have taken into our keeping
and polished with our hands belongs to a truth
greater than ours, in the animals' keeping.
Coyotes are circling around our truth.

Boom Town

Into any sound important
a snake puts out its tongue;
so at the edge of my home town
every snake listened.

And all night those oil well engines
went talking into the dark;
every beat fell through a snake,
quivering to the end.

This summer, home on a visit,
I walked out late one night;
only one hesitant pump, distant,
was remembering the past.

Often it faltered for breath
to prove how late it was;
the snakes, forgetting away through the grass,
had all closed their slim mouths.

Level Light

Sometimes the light when evening fails
stains all haystacked country and hills,
runs the cornrows and clasps the barn
with that kind of color escaped from corn
that brings to autumn the winter word—
a level shaft that tells the world:

> *It is too late now for earlier ways;*
> *now there are only some other ways,*
> *and only one way to find them—fail.*

In one stride night then takes the hill.

Ice-Fishing

Not thinking other than how the hand works
I wait until dark here on the cold
world rind, ice-curved over simplest rock,
where the tugged river flows over hidden
springs too insidious to be quite forgotten.

When the night comes I plunge my hand
where the string of fish know their share
of the minimum. Then, bringing back my hand
is a great sunburst event; and slow
home with me over unmarked snow

In the wild flipping warmth of won-back thought
my boots, my hat, my body go.

The Well Rising

The well rising without sound,
the spring on a hillside,
the plowshare brimming through deep ground
everywhere in the field—

The sharp swallows in their swerve
flaring and hesitating
hunting for the final curve
coming closer and closer—

The swallow heart from wing beat to wing beat
counseling decision, decision:
thunderous examples. I place my feet
with care in such a world.

A Ritual to Read to Each Other

If you don't know the kind of person I am
and I don't know the kind of person you are
a pattern that others made may prevail in the world
and following the wrong god home we may miss our star.

For there is many a small betrayal in the mind,
a shrug that lets the fragile sequence break
sending with shouts the horrible errors of childhood
storming out to play through the broken dyke.

And as elephants parade holding each elephant's tail,
but if one wanders the circus won't find the park,
I call it cruel and maybe the root of all cruelty
to know what occurs but not recognize the fact.

And so I appeal to a voice, to something shadowy,
a remote important region in all who talk:
though we could fool each other, we should consider—
lest the parade of our mutual life get lost in the dark.

For it is important that awake people be awake,
or a breaking line may discourage them back to sleep;
the signals we give—yes or no, or maybe—
should be clear: the darkness around us is deep.

Connections

Ours is a low, curst, under-swamp land
the raccoon puts his hand in,
gazing through his mask for tendrils
that will hold it all together.

No touch can find that thread, it is too small.
Sometimes we think we learn its course—
through evidence no court allows
a sneeze may glimpse us Paradise.

But ways without a surface we can find
flash through the mask only by surprise—
a touch of mud, a raccoon smile.

And if we purify the pond, the lilies die.

Sayings from the Northern Ice

It is people at the edge who say
things at the edge: winter is toward knowing.

Sled runners before they meet have long talk apart.
There is a pup in every litter the wolves will have.
A knife that falls points at an enemy.
Rocks in the wind know their place: down low.
Over your shoulder is God; the dying deer sees Him.

At the mouth of the long sack we fall in forever
storms brighten the spikes of the stars.

Wind that buried bear skulls north of here
and beats moth wings for help outside the door
is bringing bear skull wisdom, but do not ask the skull
too large a question till summer.
Something too dark was held in that strong bone.

Better to end with a lucky saying:

Sled runners cannot decide to join or to part.
When they decide, it is a bad day.

FROM *Traveling through the Dark* (1962)

Traveling through the Dark

Traveling through the dark I found a deer
dead on the edge of the Wilson River road.
It is usually best to roll them into the canyon:
that road is narrow; to swerve might make more dead.

By glow of the tail-light I stumbled back of the car
and stood by the heap, a doe, a recent killing;
she had stiffened already, almost cold.
I dragged her off; she was large in the belly.

My fingers touching her side brought me the reason—
her side was warm; her fawn lay there waiting,
alive, still, never to be born.
Beside that mountain road I hesitated.

The car aimed ahead its lowered parking lights;
under the hood purred the steady engine.
I stood in the glare of the warm exhaust turning red;
around our group I could hear the wilderness listen.

I thought hard for us all—my only swerving—,
then pushed her over the edge into the river.

In Medias Res

On Main one night when they sounded the chimes
my father was ahead in shadow, my son
behind coming into the streetlight, on each side
a brother and a sister; and overhead
the chimes went arching for the perfect sound.
There was a one-stride god on Main that night,
all walkers in a cloud.

I saw pictures, windows taking shoppers
where the city went, a great shield hammering out,
my wife loving the stations on that shield
and following into the shades calling back.
I had not thought to know the hero quite so well.
"Aeneas!" I cried, "just man, defender!"
And our town burned and burned.

Elegy

The responsible sound of the lawnmower
puts a net under the afternoon;
closing the refrigerator door
I hear a voice in the other room
that starts up color in every cell:
    Presents like this, Father, I got from you,
    and there are hundreds more to tell.

One night, sound held in cornfield farms
drowned in August, and melonflower breath
creeping in stealth—we walked west
where all the rest of the country slept.
I hold that memory in both my arms—
    how the families there had starved the dogs;
    in the night they waited to be fed.

At the edge of dark there paled a flash—
a train came on with its soft tread

that roused itself with light and thundered
with dragged windows curving down earth's side
while the cornstalks whispered.
　　All of us hungry creatures watched
　　until it was extinguished.

If only once in all those years
the right goodby could have been said!
I hear you climbing up the snow,
a brown-clad wanderer on the road
with the usual crooked stick,
　　and on the wrong side of the mountains
　　I can hear the latches click.

Remember in the Southwest going down the canyons?
We turned off the engine, the tires went hoarse
picking up sound out of turned away mountains;
we felt the secret sky lean down.
Suddenly the car came to with a roar.
　　And remember the Christmas wreath on our door—
　　when we threw it away and it jumped blue up the fire?

At sight of angels or anything unusual
you are to mark the spot with a cross,
for I have set out to follow you
and these marked places are expected,
but in between I can hear no sound.
　　The softest hush of doors I close
　　may jump to slam in a March wind.

When you left our house that night and went falling
into that ocean, a message came: silence.
I pictured you going, spangles and bubbles
leaving your pockets in a wheel clockwise.
Sometimes I look out of our door at night.
　　When you send messages they come spinning
　　back into sound with just leaves rustling.

Come battering. I listen, am the same, waiting.

A Stared Story

Over the hill came horsemen, horsemen whistling.
They were all hard-driven, stamp, stamp, stamp.
Legs withdrawn and delivered again like pistons,
down they rode into the winter camp,
and while earth whirled on its forgotten center
those travelers feasted till dark in the lodge of their chief.
Into the night at last on earth their mother
they drummed away; the farthest hoofbeat ceased.

Often at cutbanks where roots hold dirt together
survivors pause in the sunlight, quiet, pretending
that stared story—and gazing at earth their mother:
all journey far, hearts beating, to some such ending.
And all, slung here in our cynical constellation,
whistle the wild world, live by imagination.

Thinking for Berky

In the late night listening from bed
I have joined the ambulance or the patrol
screaming toward some drama, the kind of end
that Berky must have some day, if she isn't dead.

The wildest of all, her father and mother cruel,
farming out there beyond the old stone quarry
where highschool lovers parked their lurching cars,
Berky learned to love in that dark school.

Early her face was turned away from home
toward any hardworking place; but still her soul,
with terrible things to do, was alive, looking out
for the rescue that—surely, some day—would have to come.

Windiest nights, Berky, I have thought for you,
and no matter how lucky I've been I've touched wood.
There are things not solved in our town though tomorrow came:
there are things time passing can never make come true.

We live in an occupied country, misunderstood;
justice will take us millions of intricate moves.
Sirens will hunt down Berky, you survivors in your beds
listening through the night, so far and good.

With My Crowbar Key

I do tricks in order to know:
careless I dance,
then turn to see
the mark to turn God left for me.

Making my home in vertigo
I pray with my screams
and think with my hair
prehensile in the dark with fear.

When I hear the well bucket strike something soft
far down at noon,
then there's no place
far enough away to hide my face.

When I see my town over sights of a rifle,
and carved by light
from the lowering sun,
then my old friends darken one by one.

By step and step like a cat toward God
I dedicated walk,
but under the house
I realize the kitten's crouch.

And by night like this I turn and come
to this possible house
which I open, and see
myself at work with this crowbar key.

Parentage

My father didn't really belong in history.
He kept looking over his shoulder at some mistake.
He was a stranger to me, for I belong.

There never was a particular he couldn't understand,
but there were too many in too long a row,
and like many another he was overwhelmed.

Today drinking coffee I look over the cup
and want to have the right amount of fear,
preferring to be saved and not, like him, heroic.

I want to be as afraid as the teeth are big,
I want to be as dumb as the wise are wrong:
I'd just as soon be pushed by events to where I belong.

The Research Team in the Mountains

We have found a certain heavy kind of wolf.
Haven't seen it, though—
just *know* it.

Answers are just echoes, they say. But
a question travels before it comes back,
and that counts.

Did you know that here everything is free?
We've found days that wouldn't allow a price
on anything.

When a dirty river and a clean river
come together the result is—
dirty river.

If your policy is to be friends in the mountains
a rock falls on you: the only real friends—
you can't help it.

Many go home having "conquered a mountain"—
they leave their names at the top in a jar
for snow to remember.

Looking out over the campfire at night
again this year I pick a storm for you,
again the first one.

We climbed Lostine and Hurricane and Chief Joseph canyons;
finally in every canyon the road ends.
Above that—storms of stone.

Prairie Town

There was a river under First and Main;
the salt mines honeycombed farther down.
A wealth of sun and wind ever so strong
converged on that home town, long gone.

At the north edge there were the sandhills.
I used to stare for hours at prairie dogs,
which had their town, and folded their little paws
to stare beyond their fence where I was.

River rolling in secret, salt mines with care
holding your crystals and stillness, north prairie—
what kind of trip can I make, with what old friend,
ever to find a town so widely rich again?

Pioneers, for whom history was walking through dead grass,
and the main things that happened were miles and the time of day—
you built that town, and I have let it pass.
Little folded paws, judge me: I came away.

The Old Hamer Place

The wind came every night like an animal
rushing our house, disappearing before day,
leaving us all we could stand of the way it would be
when a hand always raised over the world fell,
or when horizontal tomorrow dimensioned out
from a scene so deep it captured our eyes.
    The animal made off thrashing limbs,
    ·taking a message in its heavy shoulders
      into the lean hills among the low stars, crashing.

All this had got lost from my mind: now
no one in all the world tonight is
even thinking about that hollow house
when the truck left years ago and the moaning
seasons began to wander through the room, stirring
vines and their shadows that grew in the dark.
    I touch that wall, collapsing it there where
      no one knows, by the quavering owl sound
      in a forest no one knows.

But the world is loaded with places for tomorrow to visit,
though this had got lost from my mind,
how the truck left years ago.
Enough air moves any morning for stillness to
come where the windows are. A place that
changed is a different place, but
    A whole town might come shuddering back, that had disappeared
    when a dark animal began to overcome the world
    and a little bird came to sing our walls down.

The Tillamook Burn

These mountains have heard God;
they burned for weeks. He spoke
in a tongue of flame from sawmill trash
and you can read His word down to the rock.

In milky rivers the steelhead
butt upstream to spawn
and find a world with depth again,
starting from stillness and water across gray stone.

Inland along the canyons
all night weather smokes
past the deer and the widow-makers—
trees too dead to fall till again He speaks,

Mowing the criss-cross trees and the listening peaks.

On Quitting a Little College

By footworn boards, by steps
that sagged years after the pride of workmen,
by things that had to *do* so long they now seemed right,
by ways of acting so old they grooved the people
(and all this among fields that never quit
under a patient sky),
I taught. And then I quit.

"Let's walk home," the president said.
He faced down the street,
and on the rollers of bird flight
through the year-round air
that little town became all it had promised him.
He could not quit; he could not let go fast enough;
his duties carried him.

The bitter habit of the forlorn cause
is my addiction. I miss it now, but face
ahead and go in my own way
toward my own place.

Reporting Back

By the secret that holds the forest up,
no one will escape. (We have reached this place.)

The sky will come home some day.
(We pay all mistakes our bodies make when they move.)

Is there a way to walk that living has obscured?
(Our feet are trying to remember some path we are walking toward.)

In Response to a Question

The earth says have a place, be what that place
requires; hear the sound the birds imply
and see as deep as ridges go behind
each other. (Some people call their scenery flat,
their only picture framed by what they know:
I think around them rise a riches and a loss
too equal for their chart—but absolutely tall.)

The earth says every summer have a ranch
that's minimum: one tree, one well, a landscape
that proclaims a universe—sermon
of the hills, hallelujah mountain,
highway guided by the way the world is tilted,
reduplication of mirage, flat evening:
a kind of ritual for the wavering.

The earth says where you live wear the kind
of color that your life is (gray shirt for me)
and by listening with the same bowed head that sings
draw all into one song, join
the sparrow on the lawn, and row that easy
way, the rage without met by the wings
within that guide you anywhere the wind blows.

Listening, I think that's what the earth says.

B.C.

The seed that met water spoke a little name.

(Great sunflowers were lording the air that day;
this was before Jesus, before Rome; that other air
was readying our hundreds of years to say things
that rain has beat down on over broken stones
and heaped behind us in many slag lands.)

Quiet in the earth a drop of water came,
and the little seed spoke: "Sequoia is my name."

Lit Instructor

Day after day up there beating my wings
with all of the softness truth requires
I feel them shrug whenever I pause:
they class my voice among tentative things,

And they credit fact, force, battering.
I dance my way toward the family of knowing,
embracing stray error as a long-lost boy
and bringing him home with my fluttering.

Every quick feather asserts a just claim;
it bites like a saw into white pine.
I communicate right; but explain to the dean—
well, Right has a long and intricate name.

And the saying of it is a lonely thing.

The Star in the Hills

A star hit in the hills behind our house
up where the grass turns brown touching the sky.

Meteors have hit the world before, but this was near,
and since TV; few saw, but many felt the shock.
The state of California owns that land
(and out from shore three miles), and any stars
that come will be roped off and viewed on week days 8 to 5.

A guard who took the oath of loyalty and denied
any police record told me this:
"If you don't have a police record yet
you could take the oath and get a job
if California should be hit by another star."

"I'd promise to be loyal to California
and to guard any stars that hit it," I said,
"or any place three miles out from shore,
unless the star was bigger than the state—
in which case, I'd be loyal to *it*."

But he said no exceptions were allowed,
and he leaned against the state-owned meteor
so calm and puffed a cork-tip cigarette
that I looked down and traced with my foot in the dust
and thought again and said, "OK—any star."

Universe Is One Place

Crisis they call it?—when
when the gentle wheat leans at the combine and
and the farm girl brings cool jugs wrapped in burlap
slapping at her legs?

We think—drinking cold water
water looking at the sky—

Sky is home, universe is one place.
Crisis? City folks make

Make such a stir.
Farm girl away through the wheat.

In the Night Desert

The Apache word for love twists
    then numbs the tongue:
Uttered once clear, said—
    never that word again.

"Cousin," you call, or "Sister" and one
    more word that spins
In the dust: a talk-flake
    chipped like obsidian.

The girl who hears this flake and
    follows you into the dark
Turns at a touch: the night desert
    forever behind her back.

Before the Big Storm

You are famous in my mind.
When anyone mentions your name
all the boxes marked "1930s"
fall off the shelves;
and the orators on the Fourth of July
all begin shouting again.
The audience of our high school commencement
begin to look out of the windows at the big storm.

And I think of you in our play—
oh, helpless and lonely!—crying,

and your father is dead again.
He was drunk; he fell.

When they mention your name,
our houses out there in the wind
creak again in the storm;
and I lean from our play, wherever I am,
to you, quiet at the edge of that town:
"All the world is blowing away."
"It is almost daylight."
"Are you warm?"

At Liberty School

Girl in the front row who had no mother
and went home every day to get supper,
the class became silent when you left early.

Elaborate histories were in our book
but of all the races you were the good:
the taxes of Rome were at your feet.

When the bell rang we did not write any more.
Traitor to everything else, we poured
to the fountain. I bent and thought of you.

Our town now is Atlantis, crystal-water-bound;
at the door of the schoolhouse fish are swimming round;
thinking in and out of the church tower go deep waves.

Girl in the front row who had no mother,
as I passed the alleys of our town toward supper
there were not spiteful nails in any board.

Lake Chelan

They call it regional, this relevance—
the deepest place we have: in this pool forms
the model of our land, a lonely one,
responsive to the wind. Everything we own
has brought us here: from here we speak.

The sun stalks among these peaks to sight
the lake down aisles, long like a gun;
a ferryboat, lost by a century, toots
for trappers, the pelt of the mountains
rinsed in the sun and that sound.

Suppose a person far off to whom this lake
occurs: told a problem, he might hear a word
so dark he drowns an instant, and stands dumb
for the centuries of his country and the suave
hills beyond the stranger's sight.

Is this man dumb, then, for whom Chelan lives
in the wilderness? On the street you've seen
someone like a trapper's child pause,
and fill his eyes with some irrelevant flood—
a tide stops him, delayed in his job.

Permissive as a beach, he turns inland,
harks like a fire, glances through the dark
like an animal drinking, and arrives along that line
a lake has found far back in the hills
where what comes finds a brim gravity exactly requires.

Fall Journey

Evening came, a paw, to the gray hut by the river.
Pushing the door with a stick, I opened it.
Only a long walk had brought me there,
steps into the continent they had placed before me.

I read weathered log, stone fireplace, broken chair,
the dead grass outside under the cottonwood tree—
and it all stared back. We've met before, my memory
started to say, somewhere. . . .

And then I stopped: my father's eyes were gray.

Late at Night

Falling separate into the dark
the hailstone yelps of geese pattered
through our roof; startled we listened.

Those V's of direction swept by unseen
so orderly that we paused. But then
faltering back through their circle they came.

Were they lost up there in the night?
They always knew the way, we thought.
You looked at me across the room:—

We live in a terrible season.

A Dedication

We stood by the library. It was an August night.
Priests and sisters of hundreds of unsaid creeds
passed us going their separate pondered roads.
We watched them cross under the corner light.

Freights on the edge of town were carrying away
flatcars of steel to be made into secret guns;
we knew, being human, that they were enemy guns,
and we were somehow vowed to poverty.

No one stopped or looked long or held out a hand.
They were following orders received from hour to hour,
so many signals, all strange, from a foreign power:
But tomorrow, you whispered, *peace may flow over the land.*

At that corner in a flash of lightning we two stood;
that glimpse we had will stare through the dark forever:
on the poorest roads we would be walkers and beggars,
toward some deathless meeting involving a crust of bread.

"The Lyf So Short . . ."

We have lived in that room larger than the world,
cage in gold, corona in the dark,
where Chaucer let the pen go its quiet work
netting Criseyde, weeping as he wrote.

That man in the monk's hood climbs through flower stems
looking up at us his condemned man's look:
on secret pilings an imagined tide goes out,
over the sky go padding feet,

While we are forced backward into our dreams.
We are all sons of medieval kings;
"*O alma redemptoris*" is a grain on our tongue,
but no saint's hand can pluck the pain from us:—

Today we have to stand in absolute rain
and face whatever comes from God,
or stoop to smooth the earth over little things
that went into dirt, out of the world.

At the Old Place

The beak of dawn's rooster pecked
in the sky, and early Ella
called us.
I awoke to worse than sleep,
saw things clear beyond the barn,
and Ella older.

That was years—barns—ago.
But should another rooster crow
I'd be more wise,
listen better in the dawn,
wake at once to more than day—
to Ella always.

Adults Only

Animals own a fur world;
people own worlds that are variously, pleasingly, bare.
And the way these worlds *are* once arrived for us kids with a jolt,
that night when the wild woman danced
in the giant cage we found we were all in
at the state fair.

Better women exist, no doubt, than that one,
and occasions more edifying, too, I suppose.
But we have to witness for ourselves what comes for us,
nor be distracted by barkers of irrelevant ware;
and a pretty good world, I say, arrived that night
when that woman came farming right out of her clothes,
by God,

At the state fair.

Glances

Two people meet. The sky turns winter,
quells whatever they would say.
Then, a periphery glance into danger—
and an avalanche already on its way.

They have been honest all of their lives;
careful, calm, never in haste;
they didn't know what it is to *meet*.
Now they have met: the world is waste.

They find they are riding an avalanche
feeling at rest, all danger gone.
The present looks out of their eyes; they stand
calm and still on a speeding stone.

Fall Wind

Pods of summer crowd around the door;
I take them in the autumn of my hands.

Last night I heard the first cold wind outside;
the wind blew soft, and yet I shiver twice:

Once for thin walls, once for the sound of time.

As Pippa Lilted

Good things will happen
when the green flame of spring
goes up into hills where
we'd have our ranch if
we had the money.

It will be soon—
we'll hold our arms ready,

long toward the table
like Cézanne's people,
and let the light pour.

Just wait a little more—
let new errors cancel
the things we did wrong.
That's the right way for us:
our errors will dance.

It will be soon;
good things will happen.

The Trip

Our car was fierce enough;
no one could tell we were only ourselves;
so we drove, equals of the car,
and ate at a drive-in where Citizens were dining.
A waitress with eyes made up to be Eyes
brought food spiced by the neon light.

Watching, we saw the manager greet people—
hollow on the outside, some kind of solid veneer.
When we got back on the road we welcomed
it as a fierce thing welcomes the cold.
Some people you meet are so dull
that you always remember their names.

Representing Far Places

In the canoe wilderness branches wait for winter;
every leaf concentrates; a drop from the paddle falls.
Up through water at the dip of a falling leaf
to the sky's drop of light or the smell of another star
fish in the lake leap arcs of realization,
hard fins prying out from the dark below.

Often in society when the talk turns witty
you think of that place, and can't polarize at all:
it would be a kind of treason. The land fans in your head
canyon by canyon; steep roads diverge.
Representing far places you stand in the room,
all that you know merely a weight in the weather.

It is all right to be simply the way you have to be,
among contradictory ridges in some crescendo of knowing.

In Fear and Valor

My mother was afraid
and in my life her fear has hid:
when Perseus holds the Gorgon's head,
she cringes, naked.

Clothed in my body, wild,
even as I grew strong,
my mother, weeping, suffered
the whole world's wrong.

Vanquished and trembling before she died,
she claimed a place in my every limb:
my mother, lost in my stride, fears Death,
as I hunt him.

At Cove on the Crooked River

At Cove at our camp in the open canyon
it was the kind of place where you might look out
some evening and see trouble walking away.

And the river there meant something
always coming from snow and flashing around boulders
after shadow-fish lurking below the mesa.

We stood with wet towels over our heads for shade,
looking past the Indian picture rock and the kind of trees
that act out whatever has happened to them.

Oh civilization, I want to carve you like this,
decisively outward the way evening comes
over that kind of twist in the scenery

When people cramp into their station wagons
and roll up the windows, and drive away.

Looking for Someone

1
Many a time driving over the Coast Range,
down the cool side—hemlock, spruce, then shore pine—
I've known something I should have said one time:
"If we hadn't met, then everything would have to change."

2
We were judged; our shadows knew our height,
and after dark, exact, the air confirmed
all with its move or stillness:
we both were trapped on an odd-shaped island.

3
Sleet persuades a traveler: I all night
know no under the earth escape
even when the sky goes back remote.
Walking till the stars forget, I look out

4
And watch the smoke at Astoria and Seaside
cringing along the coast, and barefoot gulls
designing the sand: "Go flat, go flat,"—the waves;
the little boat, the mild riding light,

5
The sand going democratic, trading places down the wind,
everything distancing away. Finding this
took all this time, and you're not even here.
Though we met, everything had to change.

Found in a Storm

A storm that needed a mountain
met it where we were:
we woke up in a gale
that was reasoning with our tent,
and all the persuaded snow
streaked along, guessing the ground.

We turned from that curtain, down.
But sometime we will turn
back to the curtain and go
by plan through an unplanned storm,
disappearing into the cold,
meanings in search of a world.

Returned to Say

When I face north a lost Cree
on some new shore puts a moccasin down,
rock in the light and noon for seeing,
he in a hurry and I beside him.

It will be a long trip; he will be a new chief;
we have drunk new water from an unnamed stream;
under little dark trees he is to find a path
we both must travel because we have met.

Henceforth we gesture even by waiting;
there is a grain of sand on his knifeblade

so small he blows it and while his breathing
darkens the steel his eyes become set

And start a new vision: the rest of his life.
We will mean what he does. Back of this page
the path turns north. We are looking for a sign.
Our moccasins do not mark the ground.

In Dear Detail, by Ideal Light

1
Night huddled our town,
plunged from the sky.
You moved away.
I save what I can of the time.

In other towns, calling my name,
home people hale me, dazed;
those moments we hold,
reciting in the evening,

Reciting about you, receding
through the huddle of any new town.
Can we rescue the light
that happened, and keeps on happening, around us?

Gradually we left you there
surrounded by the river curve
and the held-out arms,
elms under the streetlight.

These vision emergencies come
wherever we go—
blind home
coming near at unlikely places.

2

One's duty: to find a place
that grows from his part of the world—
it means leaving
certain good people.

Think: near High Trail, Colorado,
a wire follows cottonwoods
helping one to know—
like a way on trust.

That lonely strand leaves the road
depending on limbs or little poles,
and slants away,
hunting a ranch in the hills.

There, for the rest of the years,
by not going there, a person could believe
some porch looking south,
and steady in the shade—maybe you,

Rescued by how the hills
happened to arrive where they are,
depending on that wire
going to an imagined place

Where finally the way the world feels
really means how things are,
in dear detail,
by ideal light all around us.

The Wanderer Awaiting Preferment

In a world where no one knows for sure
I hold the blanket for the snow to find:
come winter, then the blizzard, then demand—
the final strategy of right, the snow
like justice over stones like bread.

"Tell us what you deserve," the whole world said.
My hands belong to cold; my voice to dust,
nobody's brother; and with a gray-eyed stare
the towns I pass return me what I give, or claim:
"Wanderer, swerve: but this is a faint command."

Only what winter gives, I claim. As trees
drink dark through roots for their peculiar grain
while meager justice applauds up through the grass,
I calm the private storm within myself.
Men should not claim, nor should they have to ask.

Vocation

This dream the world is having about itself
includes a trace on the plains of the Oregon trail,
a groove in the grass my father showed us all
one day while meadowlarks were trying to tell
something better about to happen.

I dreamed the trace to the mountains, over the hills,
and there a girl who belonged wherever she was.
But then my mother called us back to the car:
she was afraid; she always blamed the place,
the time, anything my father planned.

Now both of my parents, the long line through the plain,
the meadowlarks, the sky, the world's whole dream
remain, and I hear him say while I stand between the two,
helpless, both of them part of me:
"Your job is to find what the world is trying to be."

FROM *The Rescued Year* (1966)

Some Shadows

You would not want too reserved a speaker—
that is a cold way to live.
But where I come from withdrawal
is easy to forgive.

When Mother was a girl Indians
shadowed that country, the barren lands.
Mother ran to school winter mornings
with hot potatoes in her hands.

She was like this—foreign, a stranger.
She could not hear very well;
the world was all far. (Were the others laughing?
She never could tell.)

Later, though she was frightened,
she loved, like everyone.
A lean man, a cruel, took her.
I am his son.

He was called Hawk by the town people,
but was an ordinary man.
He lived by trapping and hunting
wherever the old slough ran.

Our house was always quiet.
Summers the windmill creaked, or a board.
I carried wood, never touching anyone.
Winters the black stove roared.

Forgive me these shadows I cling to, good people,
trying to hold quiet in my prologue.
Hawks cling the barrens wherever I live.
The world says, "Dog eat dog."

My Father: October 1942

He picks up what he thinks is
a road map, and it is
his death: he holds it easily, and
nothing can take it from his firm hand.
The pulse in his thumb on the map
says, "1:19 P.M. next Tuesday, at
this intersection." And an ambulance
begins to throb while his face looks tired.

Any time anyone may pick up something
so right that he can't put it down:
that is the problem for all who travel—they
fatally own whatever is really theirs,
and that is the inner thread, the lock,
what can hold. If it is to be, nothing breaks
it. Millions of observers guess all the
time, but each person, once, can say, "Sure."

Then he's no longer an observer. He isn't right,
or wrong. He just wins or loses.

Back Home

The girl who used to sing in the choir
would have a slow shadow on dependable walls,
I saw. We walked summer nights.
Persons came near in those days,
both afraid but not able to know
anything but a kind of Now.

In the maples an insect sang
insane for hours about how deep the dark was.
Over the river, past the light on the bridge,
and then where the light quelled at limits
in the park, we left the town,
the church lagging pretty far behind.

When I went back I saw many sharp things:
the wild hills coming to drink at the river,
the church pondering its old meanings.
I believe the hills won; I am afraid
the girl who used to sing in the choir
broke into jagged purple glass.

Across Kansas

My family slept those level miles
but like a bell rung deep till dawn
I drove down an aisle of sound,
nothing real but in the bell,
past the town where I was born.

Once you cross a land like that
you own your face more: what the light
struck told a self; every rock
denied all the rest of the world.
We stopped at Sharon Springs and ate—

My state still dark, my dream too long to tell.

A Family Turn

All her Kamikaze friends admired my aunt,
their leader, charmed in vinegar,
a woman who could blaze with such white blasts
as Lawrence's that lit Arabia.
Her mean opinions bent her hatpins.

We'd take a ride in her old car
that ripped like Sherman through society:
Main Street's oases sheltered no one
when she pulled up at Thirty-first
and whirled that Ford for another charge.

We swept headlines from under rugs, names
all over town, which I learned her way, by heart,
and blazed with love that burns because it's real.
With a turn that's our family's own,
she'd say, "Our town is not the same"—

Pause—"And it's never been."

Fifteen

South of the bridge on Seventeenth
I found back of the willows one summer
day a motorcycle with engine running
as it lay on its side, ticking over
slowly in the high grass. I was fifteen.

I admired all that pulsing gleam, the
shiny flanks, the demure headlights
fringed where it lay; I led it gently
to the road and stood with that
companion, ready and friendly. I was fifteen.

We could find the end of a road, meet
the sky on out Seventeenth. I thought about
hills, and patting the handle got back a
confident opinion. On the bridge we indulged
a forward feeling, a tremble. I was fifteen.

Thinking, back farther in the grass I found
the owner, just coming to, where he had flipped
over the rail. He had blood on his hand, was pale—
I helped him walk to his machine. He ran his hand
over it, called me good man, roared away.

I stood there, fifteen.

Homecoming

Under my hat I custom you intricate, Ella;
at homecoming I glance and remember your street.
"What happened to Ella?" they ask, asking too fast;
so I fold them off, thousands of answers deep.

"Nobody saw her after the war." We are driving;
in front of the Union Building we stop and get out.
You balanced one night on that step, then leaned.
"There's Potter's Lake." And there goes our path down straight.

"Hello, Paul." "Howdy, Tom." "Glad to see you again."
They shake. "It's been a long time," they bellow, "by God!"
I shake. They sing an old song. I hunt a face.
Every voice yells in my ear, "She's married or dead."

Oh all you revelers, back of the songs you're singing
they have torn down Ella's house—you've forgotten it;
and Ella is lost, who brightened all our class,
and I stand here, home-come, to celebrate.

Under my hat I custom you intricate, Ella,
passing the places, betraying them all with a wave,
adding past dates and jobs that led us apart
flickering into revolving doors, till I've

Lost you. What happened to Ella? Where does she live?
Remember, Tom? She's that girl we once spoke of.

The Rescued Year

Take a model of the world so big
it is the world again, pass your hand,
press back that area in the west where no one lived,
the place only your mind explores. On your thumb
that smudge becomes my ignorance, a badge
the size of Colorado: toward that state by train

we crossed our state like birds and lodged—
the year my sister gracefully
grew up—against the western boundary
where my father had a job.

Time should go the way it went
that year: we weren't at war; we had
each day a treasured unimportance;
the sky existed, so did our town;
the library had books we hadn't read;
every day at school we learned and sang,
or at least hummed and walked in the hall.

In church I heard the preacher; he said
"Honor!" with a sound like empty silos
repeating the lesson. For a minute I held
Kansas Christian all along the Santa Fe.
My father's mean attention, though, was busy—this
I knew—and going home his wonderfully level gaze
would hold the state I liked, where little happened
and much was understood. I watched my father's finger
mark off huge eye-scans of what happened in the creed.

Like him, I tried. I still try,
send my sight like a million pickpockets
up rich people's drives; it is time
when I pass for every place I go to be alive.
Around any corner my sight is a river,
and I let it arrive: rich by those brooks
his thought poured for hours
into my hand. His creed: the greatest ownership
of all is to glance around and understand.

That Christmas Mother made paper
presents; we colored them with crayons
and hung up a tumbleweed for a tree.
A man from Hugoton brought my sister
a present (his farm was tilted near oil
wells; his car ignored the little
bumps along our drive: nothing
came of all this—it was just part of the year).

I walked out where a girl I knew would be;
we crossed the plank over the ditch
to her house. There was popcorn on the stove,
and her mother recalled the old days, inviting me back.
When I walked home in the cold evening,
snow that blessed the wheat had roved
along the highway seeking furrows,
and all the houses had their lights—
oh, that year did not escape me: I rubbed
the wonderful old lamp of our dull town.

That spring we crossed the state again,
my father soothing us with stories:
the river lost in Utah, underground—
"They've explored only the ones they've found!"—
and that old man who spent his life knowing,
unable to tell how he knew—
"I've been sure by smoke, persuaded
by mist, or a cloud, or a name:
once the truth was ready"—my father smiled
at this—"it didn't care how it came."

In all his ways I hold that rescued year—
comes that smoke like love into the broken
coal, that forms to chunks again and lies
in the earth again in its dim folds, and comes a sound,
then shapes to make a whistle fade,
and in the quiet I hold no need, no hurry:
any day the dust will move, maybe settle;
the train that left will roll back into our station,
the name carved on the platform unfill with rain,
and the sound that followed the couplings back
will ripple forward and hold the train.

Judgments

I accuse—
    Ellen: you have become forty years old,
    and successful, tall, well-groomed,
    gracious, thoughtful, a secretary.
    Ellen, I accuse.

George—
    You know how to help others;
    you manage a school. You never
    let fear or pride or faltering plans
    break your control.
    George, I accuse.

I accuse—
    Tom: you have found a role;
    now you meet all kinds of people
    and let them find the truth of your
    eminence; you need not push.
    Oh, Tom, I do accuse.

Remember—
    The gawky, hardly to survive students
    we were; not one of us going to succeed,
    all of us abjectly aware of how cold,
    unmanageable the real world was?
    I remember. And that fear was true.
    And is true.

Last I accuse—
    Myself: my terrible poise, knowing
    even this, knowing that then we
    sprawled in the world
    and were ourselves part of it; now
    we hold it firmly away with gracious
    gestures (like this of mine!) we've achieved.

I see it all too well—
    And I am accused, and I accuse.

Aunt Mabel

This town is haunted by some good deed
that reappears like a country cousin, or truth
when language falters these days trying to lie,
because Aunt Mabel, an old lady gone now, would
accost even strangers to give bright flowers
away, quick as a striking snake. It's deeds like this
have weakened me, shaken by intermittent trust,
stricken with friendliness.

Our Senator talked like war, and Aunt Mabel
said, "He's a brilliant man,
but we didn't elect him that much."

Everyone's resolve weakens toward evening
or in a flash when a face melds—a stranger's, even—
reminded for an instant between menace and fear:
There are Aunt Mabels all over the world,
    or their graves in the rain.

Our City Is Guarded by Automatic Rockets

1
Breaking every law except the one
for Go, rolling its porpoise way, the rocket
staggers on its course; its feelers lock
a stranglehold ahead; and—rocking—finders
whispering "Target, Target," back and forth,
relocating all its meaning in the dark,
it freezes on the final stage. I know
that lift and pour, the flick out of the sky
and then the power. Power is not enough.

2
Bough touching bough, touching . . . till the shore,
a lake, an undecided river, and a lake again
saddling the divide: a world that won't be wise

and let alone, but instead is found outside
by little channels, linked by chance, not stern;
and then when once we're sure we hear a guide
it fades away toward the opposite end of the road
from home—the world goes wrong in order to have revenge.
Our lives are an amnesty given us.

3
There is a place behind our hill so real
it makes me turn my head, no matter. There
in the last thicket lies the cornered cat
saved by its claws, now ready to spend
all there is left of the wilderness, embracing
its blood. And that is the way that I will spit
life, at the end of any trail where I smell any hunter,
because I think our story should not end—
or go on in the dark with nobody listening.

Believer

A horse could gallop over our bridge that minnows
used for shade, but our dog trotting would splinter
that bridge—"Look down," my father said, and there
went Buster to break that bridge, but I called him back
that day:—whatever they ask me to believe, "And
        furthermore," I say.

At Niagara one night in a motel I woke, and this is what I saw—
on their little pallets all our kids lay scattered over
the floor, their dreams overcome by the story we live,
and I awake in that spell. Since then, every night
I leap through doubt, eager to find
        many more truths to tell.

And scared as I am with my blood full of sharks, I lie
in the dark and believe that whistle our dog's ears could hear
but no one else heard—it skewers my dream; and in crystals
finer than frost I trace and accept all of the ways

to know:—they tell me a lie; I don't say "But"—
    there are ways for a lie to be so.

You don't hear me yell to test the quiet or try to shake
the wall, for I understand that the wrong sound weakens
what no sound could ever save, and I am the one
to live by the hum that shivers till the world can sing:—
May my voice hover and wait for fate,
    when the right note shakes everything.

At the Chairman's Housewarming

Talk like a jellyfish can ruin a party.
It did: I smiled whatever they said,
all the time wanting to assert myself
by announcing to all, "I eat whole wheat bread."

The jelly talk stole out on the cloth
and coated the silver tine by tine,
folding meek spoons and the true knifeblades
and rolling a tentacle into the wine.

And my talk too—it poured on the table
and coiled and died in the sugar bowl,
twitching a last thin participle
to flutter the candle over its soul.

Nothing escaped the jellyfish,
that terror from seas where whales can't live
(he could kill sharks by grabbing their tails
and neither refusing nor consenting to give).

Oh go home, you terrible fish;
let sea be sea and rock be rock.
Go back wishy-washy to your sheltered bay,
but let me live definite, shock by shock.

The Epitaph Ending in And

In the last storm, when hawks
blast upward and a dove is
driven into the grass, its broken wings
a delicate design, the air between
wracked thin where it stretched before,
a clear spring bent close too often
(that Earth should ever have such wings
burnt on in blind color!), this will be
good as an epitaph:

Doves did not know where to fly, and

Keepsakes

Star Guides:
      Any star is enough
      if you know what star it is.

Kids:
      They dance before they learn
      there is anything that isn't music.

The Limbs of the Pin Oak Tree:
      "Gravity—what's that?"

An Argument Against the Empirical Method:
      Some haystacks don't even have any needle.

Comfort:
      We think it is calm here,
      or that our storm is the right size.

At This Point on the Page

Frightened at the slant of the writing, I looked up
at the student who shared it with me—
such pain was in the crossing of each t,
and a heart that skipped—lurched—in the loop of the y.
Sorrowing for the huddled lines my eyes had seen—
the terror of the o's and a's, and those draggled g's,
I looked up at her face,
not wanting to read farther, at least by prose:
the hand shook that wrote that far on the page,
and what weight formed each word, God knows.

At the Fair

Even the flaws were good—

The fat lady defining the thin man
and both bracketing the bareback princess;

Ranging through the crowd the clown
taking us all in, being extreme;

And the swain with the hangdog air
putting his trust in popcorn and cotton candy.

What more could anyone ask?
We had our money's worth.

And then besides, outside the gate,
for nothing, we met one of those lithe women—

The whirling girl, laughing with a crooked old man.

Passing Remark

In scenery I like flat country.
In life I don't like much to happen.

In personalities I like mild colorless people.
And in colors I prefer gray and brown.

My wife, a vivid girl from the mountains,
says, "Then why did you choose me?"

Mildly I lower my brown eyes—
there are so many things admirable people do not understand.

At the Klamath Berry Festival

The war chief danced the old way—
the eagle wing he held before his mouth—
and when he turned the boom-boom
stopped. He took two steps. A sociologist
was there; the Scout troop danced.
I envied him the places where he had not been.

The boom began again. Outside he heard
the stick game, and the Blackfoot gamblers
arguing at poker under lanterns.
Still-moccasined and bashful, holding
the eagle wing before his mouth,
listening and listening, he danced after others stopped.

He took two steps, the boom caught up,
the mountains rose, the still deep river
slid but never broke its quiet.
I looked back when I left:
he took two steps, he took two steps,
past the sociologist.

The Concealment: Ishi, the Last Wild Indian

A rock, a leaf, mud, even the grass
Ishi the shadow man had to put back where it was.
In order to live he had to hide that he did.
His deep canyon he kept unmarked for the world,
and only his face became lined, because no one saw it
and it therefore didn't make any difference.

If he appeared, he died; and he was the last. Erased
footprints, berries that purify the breath, rituals
before dawn with water—even the dogs roamed a land
unspoiled by Ishi who used to own it, with his aunt
and uncle, whose old limbs bound in willow bark finally
stopped and were hidden under the rocks, in sweet leaves.

We ought to help change that kind of premature suicide,
the existence gradually mottled away till the heartbeat
blends and the messages all go one way from the world
and disappear inward: Ishi lived. It was all right
for him to make a track. In California now where his opposites
unmistakably dwell we wander their streets

And sometimes whisper his name—
"Ishi."

Near

Walking along in this not quite prose way
we both know it is not quite prose we speak,
and it is time to notice this intolerable snow
innumerably touching, before we sink.

It is time to notice, I say, the freezing snow
hesitating toward us from its gray heaven;
listen—it is falling not quite silently
and under it still you and I are walking.

Maybe there are trumpets in the houses we pass
and a redbird watching from an evergreen—
but nothing will happen until we pause
to flame what we know, before any signal's given.

Recoil

The bow bent remembers home long,
the years of its tree, the whine
of wind all night conditioning
it, and its answer—Twang!

To the people here who would fret me down
their way and make me bend:
By remembering hard I could startle for home
and be myself again.

The Animal That Drank Up Sound

1
One day across the lake where echoes come now
an animal that needed sound came down. He gazed
enormously, and instead of making any, he took
away from, sound: the lake and all the land
went dumb. A fish that jumped went back like a knife,
and the water died. In all the wilderness around he
drained the rustle from the leaves into the mountainside
and folded a quilt over the rocks, getting ready
to store everything the place had known; he buried—
thousands of autumns deep—the noise that used to come there.

Then that animal wandered on and began to drink
the sound out of all the valleys—the croak of toads,
and all the little shiny noise grass blades make.
He drank till winter, and then looked out one night
at the stilled places guaranteed around by frozen
peaks and held in the shallow pools of starlight.

It was finally tall and still, and he stopped on the highest
ridge, just where the cold sky fell away
like a perpetual curve, and from there he walked on silently,
and began to starve.

When the moon drifted over the night the whole world lay
just like the moon, shining back that still
silver, and the moon saw its own animal dead
on the snow, its dark absorbent paws and quiet
muzzle, and thick, velvet, deep fur.

2
After the animal that drank sound died, the world
lay still and cold for months, and the moon yearned
and explored, letting its dead light float down
the west walls of canyons and then climb its delighted
soundless way up the east side. The moon
owned the earth its animal had faithfully explored.
The sun disregarded the life it used to warm.

But on the north side of a mountain, deep in some rocks,
a cricket slept. It had been hiding when that animal
passed, and as spring came again this cricket waited,
afraid to crawl out into the heavy stillness.
Think how deep the cricket felt, lost there
in such a silence—the grass, the leaves, the water,
the stilled animals all depending on such a little
thing. But softly it tried—"Cricket!"—and back like a river
from that one act flowed the kind of world we know,
first whisperings, then moves in the grass and leaves;
the water splashed, and a big night bird screamed.

It all returned, our precious world with its life and sound,
where sometimes loud over the hill the moon,
wild again, looks for its animal to roam, still,
down out of the hills, any time.
But somewhere a cricket waits.

It listens now, and practices at night.

FROM *Allegiances* (1970)

With Kit, Age 7, at the Beach

We would climb the highest dune,
from there to gaze and come down:
the ocean was performing;
we contributed our climb.

Waves leapfrogged and came
straight out of the storm.
What should our gaze mean?
Kit waited for me to decide.

Standing on such a hill,
what would you tell your child?
That was an absolute vista.
Those waves raced far, and cold.

"How far could you swim, Daddy,
in such a storm?"
"As far as was needed," I said,
and as I talked, I swam.

Bess

Ours are the streets where Bess first met her
cancer. She went to work every day past the
secure houses. At her job in the library
she arranged better and better flowers, and when
students asked for books her hand went out
to help. In the last year of her life
she had to keep her friends from knowing
how happy they were. She listened while they

complained about food or work or the weather.
And the great national events danced
their grotesque, fake importance. Always

Pain moved where she moved. She walked
ahead; it came. She hid; it found her.
No one ever served another so truly;
no enemy ever meant so strong a hate.
It was almost as if there was no room
left for her on earth. But she remembered
where joy used to live. She straightened its flowers;
she did not weep when she passed its houses;
and when finally she pulled into a tiny corner
and slipped from pain, her hand opened
again, and the streets opened, and she wished all well.

Holcomb, Kansas

The city man got dust on his shoes and carried
a box of dirt back to his apartment.
He joined the killers in jail and saw things
their way. He visited the scene of the crime
and backed people against the wall with his typewriter
and watched them squirm. He saw how it was.
And they—they saw how it was: he was
a young man who had wandered onto the farm
and begun to badger the homefolk.
So they told him stories for weeks while he
fermented the facts in his little notebook.

Now the wide country has gone sober again.
The river talks all through the night, proving
its gravel. The valley climbs back into its hammock
below the mountains and becomes again only what
it is: night lights on farms make little blue domes
above them, bright pools for the stars; again
people can visit each other, talk easily,
deal with real killers only when they come.

A Gesture toward an Unfound Renaissance

There was the slow girl in art class,
less able to say where our lessons led: we
learned so fast she could not follow us.
But at the door each day I looked back
at her rich distress, knowing almost enough
to find a better art inside the lesson.

And then, late at night, when the whole town
was alone, the current below the rumbly bridge
at Main Street would go an extra swirl
and gurgle, once, by the pilings;
and at my desk at home, or when our house
opened above my bed toward the stars,
I would hear that one intended lonely sound,
the signature of the day, the ratchet of time
taking me a step toward here, now, and this
look back through the door that always closes.

Reaching Out to Turn On a Light

Every lamp that approves its foot
shyly reminds of how Ellen stood.

Every bowl, every shadow that leans forth,
hunts vaguely for the pattern by her door.

One summer, I remember, a giant beautiful cloud
stood beyond the hill where Ellen lived.

It has been years, and we hardly looked back;
now, except for times like this, we hardly ever look.

There may be losses too great to understand
that rove after you and—faint and terrible—
    rip unkown through your hand.

At the Grave of My Brother

The mirror cared less and less at the last, but
the tone of his voice roamed, had more to find,
back to the year he was born; and the world
that saw him awhile again went blind.

Drawn backward along the street, he disappeared
by the cedars that faded a long time ago
near the grave where Mother's hair was a screen
but she was crying. I see a sparrow

Chubby like him, full of promise, barely
holding a branch and ready to fly.
In his house today his children begin
to recede from this year and go their own way.

Brother: Goodby.

Father's Voice

"No need to get home early;
the car can see in the dark."
        He wanted me to be rich
        the only way we could,
        easy with what we had.

And always that was his gift,
given for me ever since,
        easy gift, a wind
        that keeps on blowing for flowers
        or birds wherever I look.

World, I am your slow guest,
one of the common things
        that move in the sun and have
        close, reliable friends
        in the earth, in the air, in the rock.

A Sound from the Earth

Somewhere, I think in Dakota,
they found the leg bones—just the
big leg bones—of several hundred
buffalo, in a gravel pit.

Near there, a hole in a cliff
has been hollowed so that
the prevailing wind
thrums a note so low and persistent
that bowls of water placed in that
cave will tremble to foam.

The grandfather of Crazy Horse
lived there, they say, at the last,
and his voice like the thrum of the hills
made winter come as he sang, "Boy,
where was your buffalo medicine?
I say you were not brave enough, Boy.
I say Crazy Horse was too cautious."

Then the sound he cried out for his grandson
made that thin Agency soup that they
put before him tremble. The whole
earthen bowl churned into foam.

Stories from Kansas

Little bunches of
grass pretend they are bushes
that never will bow.
    They bow.

Carelessly the earth
escapes, loping out from the
timid little towns
    toward Colorado.

Which of the horses
we passed yesterday whinnied
all night in my dreams?
    I want that one.

Things That Happen

Sometimes before great events a person will try,
disguised, at his best, not to be a clown:
he feels, "A great event is coming, bow down."
And I, always looking for something anyway,
always bow down.

Once, later than dawn but early,
before the lines of the calendar fell,
one of those events turned an unseen corner
and came near, near, sounding before it
something the opposite from a leper's bell.

We were back of three mountains called
"Sisters" along the Green Lakes trail
and had crossed a ridge when that
one little puff of air touched us,
hardly felt at all.

That was the greatest event that day;
it righted all wrong.
I remember it, the way the dust moved there.
Something had come out of the ground
and moved calmly along.

No one was ahead of us, no one
in all that moon-like land.
Oh, I thought, how hard the world has tried
with its wind, its miles, its blundering
stumbling days, again and again, to find my hand.

Vacation Trip

The loudest sound in our car
was Mother being glum:

    Little chiding valves
    a surge of detergent oil
    all that deep chaos
    the relentless accurate fire
    the drive shaft wild to arrive

And tugging along behind in its great big
balloon,
that looming piece of her mind:

"I wish I hadn't come."

Note

straw, feathers, dust—
little things

but if they all go one way,
that's the way the wind goes.

Religion Back Home

1
When God's parachute failed,
about the spring of 1945,
the sky in Texas jerked open
and we all sailed easily
into this new strange harness on the stars.

2
The minister smoked,
and he drank,
and there was that woman in the choir,
but what really finished him—
he wore spats.

3
A Short Review of *Samson Agonistes*
   Written for Miss Arrington's Class
   in Liberal High School

Our Father Who art in Heaven
can lick their Father Who art in Heaven.

4
When my little brother chanted,
"In 1492 Jesus crossed the ocean blue,"
Mother said, "Bob, you mean
Columbus crossed the ocean blue."
And he said, "I always did get
them two guys mixed up."

Any Time

Vacation? Well, our children took our love apart:
"Why do you hold Daddy's hand?" "Susy's mother
doesn't have gray in her hair." And scenes crushed
our wonder—Sun Valley, Sawtooths, those reaches
of the Inland Passage, while the children took our
simple love apart.

(Children, how many colors does the light have?
Remember the wide shafts of sunlight, roads
through the trees, how light examines the road hour
by hour? It is all various, no simple on-off colors.
And love does not come riding west through the
trees to find you.)

"Daddy, tell me your best secret." (I have woven
a parachute out of everything broken; my scars
are my shield; and I jump, daylight or dark,
into any country, where as I descend I turn
native and stumble into terribly human speech
and wince recognition.)

"When you get old, how do you know what to do?"
(Waves will quiet, wind lull; and in that
instant I will have all the time in the world;
something deeper than birthdays will tell me all I need.)
"But will you do right?" (Children, children,
oh see that waterfall.)

At Our House

Home late, one lamp turned low,
crumpled pillow on the couch,
wet dishes in the sink (late snack),
in every child's room the checked,
slow, sure breath—

Suddenly in this doorway where I stand
in this house I see this place again,
this time the night as quiet, the house
as well secured, all breath but mine borne
gently on the air—

And where I stand, no one.

Allegiances

It is time for all the heroes to go home
if they have any, time for all of us common ones
to locate ourselves by the real things
we live by.

Far to the north, or indeed in any direction,
strange mountains and creatures have always lurked—
elves, goblins, trolls, and spiders:—we
encounter them in dread and wonder,

But once we have tasted far streams, touched the gold,
found some limit beyond the waterfall,
a season changes, and we come back, changed
but safe, quiet, grateful.

Suppose an insane wind holds all the hills
while strange beliefs whine at the traveler's ears,
we ordinary beings can cling to the earth and love
where we are, sturdy for common things.

Earth Dweller

It was all the clods at once become
precious; it was the barn, and the shed,
and the windmill, my hands, the crack
Arlie made in the ax handle: oh, let me stay
here humbly, forgotten, to rejoice in it all;
let the sun casually rise and set.
If I have not found the right place,
teach me; for somewhere inside, the clods are
vaulted mansions, lines through the barn sing
for the saints forever, the shed and windmill
rear so glorious the sun shudders like a gong.

Now I know why people worship, carry around
magic emblems, wake up talking dreams
they teach to their children: the world speaks.
The world speaks everything to us.
It is our only friend.

A Walk in the Country

To walk anywhere in the world, to live
now, to speak, to breathe a harmless
breath: what snowflake, even, may try
today so calm a life,
so mild a death?

Out in the country once,
walking the hollow night,
I felt a burden of silver come:
my back had caught moonlight
pouring through the trees like money.

That walk was late, though.
Late, I gently came into town,
and a terrible thing had happened:
the world, wide, unbearably bright,
had leaped on me. I carried mountains.

Though there was much I knew, though
kind people turned away,
I walked there ashamed—
into that still picture
to bring my fear and pain.

By dawn I felt all right;
my hair was covered with dew;
the light was bearable; the air
came still and cool.
And God had come back there
to carry the world again.

Since then, while over the world
the wind appeals events,
and people contend like fools,
like a stubborn tumbleweed I hold,
hold where I live, and look into every face:

Oh friends, where can one find a partner
for the long dance over the fields?

So Long

At least at night, a streetlight
is better than a star.
and better good shoes on a
long walk, than a good friend.

Often in winter with my old
cap I slip away into the gloom
like a happy fish, at home
with all I touch, at the level of love.

No one can surface till far,
far on, and all that we'll have
to love may be what's near
in the cold, even then.

FROM *Someday, Maybe* (1973)

An Introduction to Some Poems

Look: no one ever promised for sure
that we would sing. We have decided
to moan. In a strange dance that
we don't understand till we do it, we
have to carry on.

Just as in sleep you have to dream
the exact dream to round out your life,
so we have to live that dream into stories
and hold them close at you, close at the
edge we share, to be right.

We find it an awful thing to meet people,
serious or not, who have turned into vacant
effective people, so far lost that they
won't believe their own feelings
enough to follow them out.

The authentic is a line from one thing
along to the next; it interests us.
Strangely, it relates to what works,
but is not quite the same. It never
swerves for revenge,

Or profit, or fame: it holds
together something more than the world,
this line. And we are your wavery
efforts at following it. Are you coming?
Good: now it is time.

Thirteenth and Pennsylvania

Motorcycle, count my sins.
Pull away fast, drown them far.

Reverse my glance, blank windows; hold
sunset by the light in the sky.

Foot on the curb, reject what was.
By your thousands, people, absolve this man.

I glance my path into that deep frame
where wanderers plunge. I beg of the wind:

Read my lips, forget my name.

New Letters from Thomas Jefferson

Dear Sir:

In Washington we are breathing very sincerely.

Very sincerely,
Thomas Jefferson

Dear Friend:

I give you *The Faith of the Young*: Earlier generations were more limited and selfish than the young generation. They polluted the world, oppressed the weak, indulged hypocritically in alcohol and food, flaunted their styles as superior (certain decorums in dress and speech). Remnants of that generation can be identified (besides by their age) by their callousness and arrogance. They do not have interesting ideas or life styles or tastes. They are cruel and dishonest. The governments they maintained or tolerated were oppressive and corrupt.

Very sincerely,
Thomas Jefferson

My Friend, Dear Friend,

It is like the common wind that touches you by chance at your window, our stupendous coincidence: to be alive at the same time. Being contemporaries, having this common disability, we must endure together. I lift this day and carry it carefully west, lay it at your door. It is an instant heirloom so precious that the whole sky closes on its gray edge. Everything in the world has been caught in the scene we happen to share. Through all that calendar filigree stronger than steel I speak to you, on this island that is caving toward us all around, dear friend, my friend.

Yours,
Thomas Jefferson

George W., Sir:

This turn has become the way: wait when acting; add one further turn. Hidden by time there lives this extra advantage, coiled and elegant. Our choices now disguise, wait for what the world wants—old courtesy, new strategy. We follow by going ahead of what we know is coming.

By hand—
Thomas Jefferson

From Monticello

My Old Friend,

   This morning the bees were swarming in the window well of the washroom. Birds were hunting each other. The root of the big yellow poplar was holding quiet as ever. Despite what we know and have done, I felt limited, alone. Across the morning light, particles were signaling what I cannot see.

As ever,
Thomas Jefferson

Waking at 3 A.M.

Even in the cave of the night when you
wake and are free and lonely,
neglected by others, discarded, loved only
by what doesn't matter—even in that
big room no one can see,
you push with your eyes till forever
comes in its twisted figure eight
and lies down in your head.

You think water in the river;
you think slower than the tide in
the grain of the wood; you become
a secret storehouse that saves the country,
so open and foolish and empty.

You look over all that the darkness
ripples across. More than has ever
been found comforts you. You open your
eyes in a vault that unlocks as fast
and as far as your thought can run.
A great snug wall goes around everything,
has always been there, will always
remain. It is a good world to be
lost in. It comforts you. It is
all right. And you sleep.

A Little Gift

Fur came near, night inside it,
four legs at a time, when the circus
walked off the train. From cage to cage
we carried night back to the cats and poured
it into their eyes, from ours. They
lapped steadily, and the sponge of their feet
swelled into the ground. Even today
I keep that gift: I let any next thing fold
quietly into the blackness that leads
all the way inward from the hole in my eye.

Existences

Half-wild, I hear a wolf,
half-tame, I bark. Then
in the dark I feel my master's
hand, and lick, then bite.

I envy leaves, their touch: miles
by the million, tongues everywhere
saying yea, for the forest,
and in the night, for us.

At caves in the desert, close
to rocks, I wait. I live
by grace of shadows. In moonlight
I hear a room open behind me.

At the last when you come
I am a track in the dust.

Father and Son

No sound—a spell—on, on out
where the wind went, our kite sent back
its thrill along the string that
sagged but sang and said, "I'm here!
I'm here!"—till broke somewhere,
gone years ago, but sailed forever clear
of earth. I hold—whatever tugs
the other end—I hold that string.

Indian Caves in the Dry Country

These are some canyons
we might use again
sometime.

People of the South Wind

1
One day Sun found a new canyon.
It hid for miles and ran far away,
then it went under a mountain. Now Sun
goes over but knows it is there. And that
is why Sun shines—it is always looking.
Be like the sun.

2
Your breath has a little shape—
you can see it cold days. Well,
every day it is like that, even in summer.
Well, your breath goes, a whole
army of little shapes. They are living
in the woods now and are your friends.
When you die—well, you go with

your last breath and find the others.
And in open places in the woods
all of you are together and happy.

3

Sometimes if a man is evil his breath
runs away and hides from him. When he
dies his last breath cannot find the others,
and he never comes together again—
those little breaths, you know, in the autumn
they scurry the bushes before snow.
They never come back.

4

You know where the main river
runs—well, for five days below is
No One, and out in the desert
on each side his children live.
They have their tents that echo dust
and give a call for their father
when you knock for acquaintance:
"No One, No One, No One."

When you cross that land the sandbars
have his name in little tracks
the mice inscribe under the bushes,
and on pools you read his wide, bland
reply to all that you ask. You wake
from dreams and hear the end of things:
"No One, No One, No One."

Bring the North

Mushroom, Soft Ear, Old Memory,
Root Come to Tell the Air:
bring the Forest Floor along
the valley; bring all that comes
blue into passes, long shores

around a lake, talk, talk, talk,
miles, then deep. Bring that story.

Unfold a pack by someone's door—
wrapped in leather, brought in brown,
what the miles collect.
Leave sound in an empty
house in its own room there,
a little cube hung like a birdcage
in the attic, with a swinging door.
Search out a den: try natural,
no one's, your own, a dirt
floor. Accept them all.

One way to find your place is like
the rain, a million requests
for lodging, one that wins, finds
your cheek: you find your home,
a storm that walks the waves.
You hear that cloak whip, those
chilly hands take night apart.
In split Heaven you see one sudden
eye on yours, and yours in it,
scared, falling, fallen.

Mushroom, Soft Ear, Memory,
attend what is.
Bring the North.

Report to Crazy Horse

All the Sioux were defeated. Our clan
got poor, but a few got richer.
They fought two wars. I did not
take part. No one remembers your vision
or even your real name. Now
the children go to town and like
loud music. I married a Christian.

Crazy Horse, it is not fair
to hide a new vision from you.
In our schools we are learning
to take aim when we talk, and we have
found out our enemies. They shift when
words do; they even change and hide
in every person. A teacher here says
hurt or scorned people are places
where real enemies hide. He says
we should not hurt or scorn anyone,
but help them. And I will tell you
in a brave way, the way Crazy Horse
talked: that teacher is right.

I will tell you a strange thing:
at the rodeo, close to the grandstand,
I saw a farm lady scared by a blown
piece of paper; and at that place
horses and policemen were no longer
frightening, but suffering faces were,
and the hunched-over backs of the old.

Crazy Horse, tell me if I am right:
these are the things we thought we were
doing something about.

In your life you saw many strange things,
and I will tell you another: now I salute
the white man's flag. But when I salute
I hold my hand alertly on the heartbeat
and remember all of us and how we depend
on a steady pulse together. There are those
who salute because they fear other flags
or mean to use ours to chase them:
I must not allow my part of saluting
to mean this. All of our promises,
our generous sayings to each other, our
honorable intentions—those I affirm
when I salute. At these times it is like
shutting my eyes and joining a religious

colony at prayer in the gray dawn
in the deep aisles of a church.

Now I have told you about new times.
Yes, I know others will report
different things. They have been caught
by weak ways. I tell you straight
the way it is now, and it is our way,
the way we were trying to find.

The chokecherries along our valley
still bear a bright fruit. There is good
pottery clay north of here. I remember
our old places. When I pass the Musselshell
I run my hand along those old grooves in the rock.

Deer Stolen

Deer have stood around our house
at night so still nobody knew,
and waited with ears baling air.
I hunt the still deer everywhere,

For what they heard and took away,
stepping through the chaparral,
was the sound of Then; now it's Now,
and those small deer far in the wild

Are whispers of our former life.
the last print of some small deer's foot
might hold the way, might be a start
that means in ways beyond our ken

Important things. I follow them
through all the hush of long ago
to listen for what small deer know.

The Little Ways That Encourage Good Fortune

Wisdom is having things right in your life
and knowing why.
If you do not have things right in your life
you will be overwhelmed:
you may be heroic, but you will not be wise.
If you have things right in your life
but do not know why,
you are just lucky, and you will not move
in the little ways that encourage good fortune.

The saddest are those not right in their lives
who are acting to make things right for others:
they act only from the self—
and that self will never be right:
no luck, no help, no wisdom.

The Swerve

Halfway across a bridge one night
my father's car went blind. He guided
it on by no star but a light he kept in mind.

Halfway to here, my father died.
He looked at me. He closed his eyes.
The world stayed still. Today I hold in mind

The things he said, my children's lives—
any light. Oh, any light.

Report from a Far Place

Making these word things to
step on across the world, I
could call them snowshoes.

They creak, sag, bend, but
hold, over the great deep cold,
and they turn up at the toes.

In war or city or camp
they could save your life;
you can muse them by the fire.

Be careful, though: they
burn, or don't burn, in their own
strange way, when you say them.

Freedom

Freedom is not following a river.
Freedom is following a river,
    though, if you want to.
It is deciding now by what happens now.
It is knowing that luck makes a difference.

No leader is free; no follower is free—
    the rest of us can often be free.
Most of the world are living by
creeds too odd, chancy, and habit-forming
    to be worth arguing about by reason.

If you are oppressed, wake up about
four in the morning: most places,
you can usually be free some of the time
    if you wake up before other people.

People Who Went By in Winter

The morning man came in to report
that something had crossed the field
in the night during the storm. He heard
ribbons of wind snap at their tether
and a sound like some rider saying
the ritual for help, a chant or a song.
When we went out all we found
were deep, slow tracks in freezing mud
and some sticks tied together hanging
from the lowest branch of the oldest
tree by the river.

While beginning snow eddied and curtained
thicker and thicker on, we looked.
The grass hurried by, seething, then silent,
brown, all the way to the west, a little
touch-by-touch trail to the mountains.
Our boss turned back: "No.
We can't help them. They sing till
they find a place to winter. They have
tents. They make it, somehow." He
looked off that long way, where
the grass tossed.

Riding home, he told us:
"My people were like them,
over around Grand Prairie—slaves once,
then landowners. Now they pass like
this, and I hear them, because
I wake up and am partly theirs."
He looked at every man, and
he put his hand on the neck of his horse:
"They are our people, yours and mine,
all of us," he said.
"In every storm I hear them pass."

Witness

This is the hand I dipped in the Missouri
above Council Bluffs and found the springs.
All through the days of my life I escort
this hand. Where would the Missouri
meet a kinder friend?

On top of Fort Rock in the sun I spread
these fingers to hold the world in the wind;
along that cliff, in that old cave
where men used to live, I grubbed in the dirt
for those cool springs again.

Summits in the Rockies received this diplomat.
Brush that concealed the lost children yielded
them to this hand. Even on the last morning
when we all tremble and lose, I will reach
carefully, eagerly through that rain, at the end—

Toward whatever is there, with this loyal hand.

A Song in the Manner of Flannery O'Connor

Snow on the mountain—water in
the valley: you beat a mule and
it works hard, Honey.
    Have a cigarette?

Where is the guidepost? Written on
your hand: you point places with it
and everyone understands.
    Like to dance, Honey?

Country folks used to talk to us
like this. Now they're wiser
than the rest of us.
    So long, Sucker.

Juncos

They operate from elsewhere,
some hall in the mountains—
quick visit, gone.
Specialists on branch ends,
craft union. I like their
clean little coveralls.

Why the Sun Comes Up

SELECTIONS FROM

Smoke's Way (1983)

My Name Is William Tell (1992)

Even in Quiet Places (1996)

and other volumes (1980–1993)

FROM *Smoke's Way* (1983)

Storm Warning

Something not the wind shakes along far
like a sky truck in low gear
over Oregon. Like the shore wind baying along through fir
but not now the wind, no, not really so,
it is a new weight and force
that begins to blow.

This winter they'll still call it wind and let it explore;
and when they talk it over next summer there by the shore,
along through the scrub and salal the new something will range.
In a hurry, late, it won't wait for the air.

In the fall again they'll remember, each of them, back to now.
They'll no longer call it wind, they'll want it all changed.
They'll want it all different then, but they won't know how.

R$_x$ Creative Writing: Identity

You take this pill, a new world
springs out of whatever sea
most drowned the old one,
arrives like light.

Then that bone light belongs
inside of things. You touch
or hear so much *yourself*
there is no dark,

Nothing left but what Aquinas
counted: he—touched, luminous—
bowed over sacred worlds, each one
conceived, then really there—

Not just hard things: down on
a duck as real as steel.
You know so sure there burns
a central vividness.

It tells you;
all you do is tell about it.

Survival

Evenings, we call quail.
The desert sends those lightfoot troops
against us down the trail.

So straight they tread their path,
so small, so soft, birdshot at twenty yards
for them is death.

Or step, step toward a noose
we lightly pray them on,
and let our starved eyes choose.

Then more world than they knew—more night—
comes down. For you, survivors, for you,
I shoot in this tricky light.

The Coyote in the Zoo

A yellow eye meets mine;
I suddenly know, too late,
the land outside belongs
to the one that looks away.

The Indian Cave Jerry Ramsey Found

Brown, brittle, wait-a-bit weeds
block the entrance. I untangle their
whole summer embrace. Inside—soot from
a cold fire, powder of bones,
a piece of ceremonial horn: cool
history comes off on my hands.
Outside, I stand in a canyon so
quiet its pool almost remembers its
old reflections. And then I breathe.

Meditation

Animals full of light
walk through the forest
toward someone aiming a gun
loaded with darkness.

That's the world: God
holding still
letting it happen again,
and again and again.

West of Here

The road goes down. It stops at the sea.
The sea goes on. It stops at the sky.
the sky goes on.

At the end of the road—picnickers,
rocks. We stand and look out:

Another sky where this one ends?
And another sea?
And a world, and a road?

And what about you?
And what about me?

Many Things Are Hidden by the Light

Now I remember, letting the dark
flood in, how we used to shoot animals,
and how they were afraid. We stared
into hedges. What we saw we killed.

Now I know by the cold: at night those hedges
run the crazy fields and we children of light
stagger and flash, lost where we triumph,
reeling our steadiness toward our terrible homes.

Cave Painting

It was like the moon, the open before us,
when we came out of the last hills
we had to cross, to be tracked by the stars.
And whatever we said, we knew could be heard.
Then, we learned about caves, where you have
now discovered us, even these places. But
for awhile we painted our hidden lives
deep here, and we always tried—like
this I am doing now—to find ways
even deeper, with rooms that would
blaze only for us and those of our kind.
And even now—because a picture is a disguise—
you may never know our ultimate home with
Earth over it, and the silence where without
power or worth—with nothing—we first
learned to huddle together and foil the stars.

By the Deschutes Shore

Millions of miles away at evening the sun
touches the little folded hands of the dead
mouse in the grass church by the river.
No tuft but gains a halo in the service, no
rock unwarmed. Having no hands, the world
learns everything by shouldering down in the
dusk and waiting like this while the sun
repeats its lesson color by color toward
the brown mouse, brown paws, brown, brown grass.

Gutters of Jackson: Cache Street North

Gum wrappers with nothing, Coors can
(flat), spilled—raspberry?—ice cream,
little torn flag, incredibly smashed pine
cone, Bud bottle half full of—maybe—
beer, gravel, gravel, piece of a
sign—"meet you at M. . . ."—big
baked truck tread tracks in dried mud
climbing the curb, and across from the giant
timbers of the Chamber of Commerce, just where
town hesitates before the swooping scene,
one tiny shard of glass, blue, so
intense it shines like the Pharaoh's eyes
in the dark when they closed his tomb.

Assurance

You will never be alone, you hear so deep
a sound when autumn comes. Yellow
pulls across the hills and thrums,
or the silence after lightning before it says
its names—and then the clouds' wide-mouthed
apologies. You were aimed from birth:

you will never be alone. Rain
will come, a gutter filled, an Amazon,
long aisles—you never heard so deep a sound,
moss on rock, and years. You turn your head—
that's what the silence meant: *you're not alone.*
The whole wide world pours down.

Looking for You

Looking for you through the gray rain,
your whole house is a face, windows
for eyes, door for a mouth. Chimney
breathing, your house waits. You
come down the street: you get a stare,
straight and slow to change.

No matter how willing and weak your own
face is, you know another face
for you, somewhere in the world: your house,
or a stone you choose on a mountain, or even
the wrinkled sea and its friend the wind.

Far away on an island off Alaska
there's a village gone back to forest,
and there leaning and peering—totem poles,
gray cedar eyes, crest, beak:
all those faces at home, staring from shadows,

Looking for you through the gray rain.

Smoke

Smoke's way's a good way—find,
or be rebuffed and gone:
a day and a day, the whole world home.

Smoke? Into the mountains I guess
a long time ago. Once here, yes,
everywhere. Say anything? No.

I saw Smoke, slow traveler, reluctant
but sure. Hesitant sometimes, yes,
because that's the way things are.

Smoke never doubts though:
some new move will appear.
Wherever you are, there is another door.

FROM *My Name Is William Tell* (1992)

My Name Is William Tell

My name is William Tell:
when little oppressions touch me
arrows hidden in my cloak
whisper, "Ready, ready."

At Lascaux

It came into my mind that no one had painted
there deep in the ground: if I made a beast,
an arrow into the heart, then aboveground
it would come into my mind again, and
what I hunted, wherever it was, would fall.

Now where I go, daylight or dark,
I hold something still. Before I shoot,
whatever the bow does, and the arrow, and I and
the animal, all come true down deep in the earth:
all that I am comes into my mind.

They Carved an Animal

In a cave somewhere they carved an animal
jumping: that leap stayed. Across the world
in other caves a light gleamed, once.

I stand on a porch under the rain,
and somewhere, you on yours—the rest
of the world leans out, an animal stilled.

There's a leap that lasts in every cave,
but things go on: lights pull into the stars,
a forest springs, I hear the rain.

I touch old boards.

Coyote

My left hind-
foot
        steps
in the track of my right
fore-
        foot
and my hind-right
foot
        steps
in the track of my
fore-left
        foot
and so on, for miles—

Me paying no attention, while
my nose rides along letting
the full report, the
whole blast of the countryside
come along toward me
on rollers of scent, and—

I come home with a chicken or
a rabbit and sit up
singing all night with my friends.
It's baroque, my life, and
I tell it on the mountain.

I wouldn't trade it for yours.

Inheriting the Earth: Quail

You are supposed to stay still. It won't
always save you, but sometimes it will.
And anyway, little quail, your job is
to go out there and lose, when the time comes.
For awhile you're to call to each other
and scurry for grain. You're to
fly up like a bomb. Learn from their fire
not to make any noise when you die, just
be there—be the evening.
Others have burdens of their own: everyone
does. When you stir at night you can feel
your enemies pray—necessity holding their paws
in its grip, and their own kind of pain in their eyes.

Roll Call

Red Wolf came, and Passenger Pigeon,
the Dodo Bird, all the gone or endangered
came and crowded around in a circle,
the Bison, the Irish Elk, waited
silent, the Great White Bear, fluid and strong,
sliding from the sea, streaming and creeping
in the gathering darkness, nose down,
bowing to earth its tapered head,
where the Black-footed Ferret, paws folded,
stood in the center surveying the multitude
and spoke for us all: "Dearly beloved," it said.

.38

This metal has come to look at
your eye. Look at its eye—that
stare that can't lose.

There's no grin like a gun—
as if only its calm
could soothe your hand.

But metal is cold,
cold. In the night, in the risk,
it's a touch of the dead.

It's a cold world.

Together Again

When I drive, every bridge is
a gift, and the power that swoops
the wires is ready to let go.
The little car radio drinks and drinks
whatever comes out of the sky.

Were our lost ones ever to come
home, and be hale, all four of my
own would come, the center a place
again and the hiss of the river past
a bit of grass the only sound, our whole lives—

And drama enough, this time.

Stereopticon

This can happen. They can bring the leaves back
to the cottonwood trees, those great big rooms
where our street—as long as summer—led
to the river. From a rusty nail in the alley
someone can die, but the street go on again.

Hitler and others, those pipsqueak voices,
can twitter from speakers. I can look back
from hills beyond town, and every person
and all the alleys, and even the buildings
except the church be hidden in leaves.

This can happen, my parents laughing
because they have already won. And I can
study and grow up and look back and call "Wait!"
and run after their old green car
and be lost again.

Why I Am a Poet

My father's gravestone said, "I knew it was time."
Our house was alive. It moved,
it had a song. The singers back home
all stood in rows along the railroad line.

When the wind came along the track
every neighbor sang. In the last
house I followed the wind—it
left the world and went on.

We knew, the wind and I, that space
ahead of us, the world like an empty room.
I looked back where the sky came down.
Some days no train would come.

Some birds didn't have a song.

Atwater Kent

Late nights the world flooded our dark house
in a dim throbbing from a glowing little box, velvety
sound hovering from horns, or Cab Calloway
far in a night club stretched all the way to Kansas.

Maybe rewarded with popcorn or fudge, maybe
just exhausted by the day, we sprawled on the living room
rug and were carried above our house, out
over town, and spread thin by a violin.

Once from Chicago Enio Bolognini
civilized with his cello a whole
hemisphere, and we were transformed into Italians
or other great people, listening in palaces.

Rich in our darkness, we lay inheriting
rivers of swirling millions, and the promise of never
a war again. It all came from the sky,
Heaven: London, Rome, Copenhagen.

That Year

The last year I was your friend, they fell
for days "headlong flaming down"—the leaves,
I mean. Aspens heard the news. On the deck
the birdseed sprouted—blue and brown
and rose: two evening grosbeaks came,
trim and ordered, quiet colored,
like Marines. We stood each alone:
the grass had found a tide but we felt none.

When they hurt enough, we let them out—
the words, I mean—and let them trigger
our tongues till they lugered a million times,
like a drum, till the world reversed and leaped,
after its good name. But sunset frisked us for

anything dry or warm, and that year we stood alone:
the grass had found a tide but we felt none.

That year when I was your friend—in words,
I mean—I was afraid. Despite our care
we heard the news. It was more than words.
Persuaded like the grass, we felt the tide
at last: we knew before we were told,
and we shook as the aspens did,
from a storm inside the world.

In Hurricane Canyon

After we talked, after the moon
rose, before we went to bed, we
sat quietly. That was when
we heard the river, big stones
bumping along the bottom from
away up the mountain.

How terribly shredded and lonely
the water went as it cried out and
held splinters of moonlight, and its
life raced powerfully on! That night,
we bowed, shadowed our eyes,
and followed—all the way down—
one, slow, helpless, bumping stone.

Widow

On the first day when light came through the curtain
a mosquito thought was bothering her—what if
I am important? She wandered the house—the forgiving
table, the surprised-looking bed. Dishes
in the rack needed putting away, and she helped
them. But afterward she regretted—maybe nothing
should move, maybe this day the stillness begins.

She looked out a front window and held every
neighborhood shadow exactly where it was. Then
she carefully X'd out the calendar that had waited
all year for this date. She held out her hand
in a shaft of sun and flexed her fingers, in case
time had passed, in case her body was already gone.

Vocatus atque Non Vocatus

1

Before life was there a world?
When we take our life away, will fear
be anywhere—the cold? the wind? those noises
darkness tries? We'll take fear
with us. It rides the vast night
carried in our breast. Then, everywhere—
nothing?—the way it was again?

2

Across a desert, beyond storms
and waiting, air began to make
a wing, first leather stretched on bone
extended outward, shadow-quiet,
then whispering feathers lapped against
each other, and last the air itself,
life taken back, a knife of nothing.

3

There was a call one night, and a call
back. It made a song. All
the birds waited—the sound they tried for
now over, and the turning of the world
going on in silence. Behind what happens
there is that stillness, the wings that wait,
the things to try, the wondering, the music.

One Man

"Dull Knife," that sound, his name, surrounded
what the wind recovered when it came back
searching over the grass. The bodies had
disappeared, but in his deaf ear the story
found its way, telling itself more slowly than
his life lived: that air talked on after
his tongue was gone, and this world can never
recapture its failure to say that name,
gaining always on history and racing forth
the way it broke through the cavalry that day
he died and escaped and began to wander the earth.

At Fort Worden: Calling Names

This gun emplacement where we live aims
out there, somewhere—the enemy. We stare
down a barrel where in shadow someone
stands, our president, ready to kill
someone, the enemy. I forget which ones.

These tranquil waters cuddle a shape so hot
its shadow burns your soul, a submarine
that spurns the land. We own it. It prowls
waiting to incinerate what people
we choose. "Our Buchenwald," a fractious bishop
in Seattle calls it—more fire than all the death camps
used. In darkness it glides by.

Our navy wanted to call it *Corpus Christi*.
It slips through Hood Canal.
The Duckabush, the Hama Hama, the Lilliwaup
all wash as well as they can—but there, more fire
than all the death camps patrols the world.
Sleep well, America. The body of Christ glides by,

In our name.

Dropout

Grundy and Hoagland and all the rest who ganged
our class and wrecked the high school gym for fun—
you thought of them last night, and how they laughed
when they beat up a Mexican.

Later they marched against Hitler youth, but admired
them too—how they were brave and sang: "Why,
you should see how those troopers fought!" And Hoagland
came home to a job with the FBI.

Remember the team?—the celebration in the Lions
Hall?—with Coach Gist there, a real man?—
the speeches?—the jackrabbit chile? You looked through the smoke
and the smoky jokes, and vomited.

And never went back again.

Some Remarks When Richard Hugo Came

Some war, I bomb their towns from five
miles high, the flower of smoke and fire
so far there is no sound. No cry
disturbs the calm through which we fly.

Some day, a quiet day, I watch
a grassy field in wind, the waves
forever bounding past and gone.
Friends call: I cannot look away—

And my life had already happened:
Some saved-up feeling caught, held on,
and shook me. Long-legged grass raced out;
a film inside my head unwound.

The bodies I had killed began to scream.

A Wind from a Wing

Something outside my window in the dark
whispers a message. Maybe it is
a prayer sent by one of those friends
forgiving me the years when I sat out their war.
It flared, you know, generating
its own reasons for being, its heroes
anyone killed by an enemy. They looked up
and met fame on a bullet awarded so fast
their souls remained stuck in their bodies,
and then their names, caught on flypaper
citation, couldn't escape. Their families eat that
carrion, and like it. That is their punishment.

In a sky as distant and clear as Pascal's
nightmare, and immediate as our sweat
when God shakes us from sleep, my fate
shudders me awake. Little squeals
of the unborn fly past in the wind. It is midnight
and a motel, and nobody but me remembers
my mother, my father, and that hidden key
they left by our door when I was out late.

The Gift

Time wants to show you a different country. It's the one
that your life conceals, the one waiting outside
when curtains are drawn, the one Grandmother hinted at
in her crochet design, the one almost found
over at the edge of the music, after the sermon.

It's the way life is, and you have it, a few years given.
You get killed now and then, violated
in various ways. (And sometimes it's turn about.)
You get tired of that. Long-suffering, you wait
and pray, and maybe good things come—maybe

the hurt slackens and you hardly feel it any more.
You have a breath without pain. It is called happiness.

It's a balance, the taking and passing along,
the composting of where you've been and how people
and weather treated you. It's a country where
you already are, bringing where you have been.
Time offers this gift in its millions of ways,
turning the world, moving the air, calling,
every morning, "Here, take it, it's yours."

FROM *Even in Quiet Places* (1996)

History Display

Think of those generals at the wax museum,
and the women not present, but they're somewhere,
and all the histories those people escaped by being
in the one they were in. For an instant their wars
didn't happen and a heavy sweetness comes in the air,
like flowers without any cemetery, like my sister
holding her doll up to the window before
anyone told us about the rest of the world.

Those great people can stay where they are.
With love I erase our house and bend over our town
till the streets go dim and the courthouse begins
to dissolve quietly into its lilac hedge.
Some things are made out of rock, but some
don't have to be hard. They can hold it all still,
past and future at once, now, here.

Spirit of Place: Great Blue Heron

Out of their loneliness for each other
two reeds, or maybe two shadows, lurch
forward and become suddenly a life
lifted from dawn or the rain. It is
the wilderness come back again, a lagoon
with our city reflected in its eye.
We live by faith in such presences. .

It is a test for us, that thin
but real, undulating figure that promises,
"If you keep faith I will exist
at the edge, where your vision joins
the sunlight and the rain: heads in the light,
feet that go down in the mud where the truth is."

Over in Montana

Winter stops by for a visit each year.
Dead leaves cluster around. They know what is
coming. They listen to some silent song.

At a bend in the Missouri, up where
it's clear, teal and mallards lower
their wings and come gliding in.

A cottonwood grove gets ready. Limbs
reach out. They touch and shiver.
These nights are going to get cold.

Stars will sharpen and glitter. They make
their strange signs in a rigid pattern
above hollow trees and burrows and houses—

The great story weaves closer and closer, millions of
touches, wide spaces lying out in the open,
huddles of brush and grass, all the little lives.

A Farewell, Age Ten

While its owner looks away I touch the rabbit.
Its long soft ears fold back under my hand.
Miles of yellow wheat bend; their leaves
rustle away and wait for the sun and wind.

This day belongs to my uncle. This is his farm.
We have stopped on our journey; when my father says to
we will go on, leaving this paradise, leaving
the family place. We have my father's job.

Like him, I will be strong all of my life.
We are men. If we squint our eyes in the sun
we will see far. I'm ready. It's good, this resolve.
But I will never pet the rabbit again.

Old Prof

He wants to go north. His life has become
observations about what others
have said, and he wants to go north. Up there
far enough you might hear the world, not
what people say. Maybe a road will discover
those reasons that the real travelers had.

Sometimes he looks at the map above
Moose Jaw and thinks about silence up there.
Late at night he opens an atlas
and follows the last road, then hovers
at a ghost town, letting the snow have whatever
it wants. Silence extends farther
and farther, till dawn finds the same page
and nothing has moved all night, except
that his head has bowed and rested on his arms.

Rousing to get started, he has his coffee.
He sets forth toward class. Instead of the north,
he lets an aspirin whisper through his veins.

Poetry

Its door opens near. It's a shrine
by the road, it's a flower in the parking lot
of The Pentagon, it says, "Look around,
listen. Feel the air." It interrupts
international telephone lines with a tune.
When traffic lines jam, it gets out
and dances on the bridge. If great people
get distracted by fame they forget
this essential kind of breathing
and they die inside their gold shell.
When caravans cross deserts
it is the secret treasure hidden under the jewels.

Sometimes commanders take us over, and they
try to impose their whole universe,
how to succeed by daily calculation:
I can't eat that bread.

In The Book

A hand appears.
It writes on the wall.
Just a hand moving in the air,
and writing on the wall.

A voice comes and says the words,
"You have been weighed,
you have been judged,
and have failed."

The hand disappears, the voice
fades away into silence.
And a spirit stirs and fills
the room, all space, all things.

All this in The Book
asks, "What have you done wrong?"

But The Spirit says,
"Come to me, who need comfort."

And the hand, the wall, the voice
are gone, but The Spirit is everywhere.
The story ends inside the book,
but outside, wherever you are—

It goes on.

Grace Abounding

Air crowds into my cell so considerately
that the jailer forgets this kind of gift
and thinks I'm alone. Such unnoticed largesse
smuggled by day floods over me,
or here come grass, turns in the road,
a branch or stone significantly strewn
where it wouldn't need to be.

Such times abide for a pilgrim, who all through
a story or a life may live in grace, that blind
benevolent side of even the fiercest world,
and might—even in oppression or neglect—
not care if it's friend or enemy, caught up
in a dance where no one feels need or fear:

I'm saved in this big world by unforeseen
friends, or times when only a glance
from a passenger beside me, or just the tired
branch of a willow inclining toward earth,
may teach me how to join earth and sky.

Men

After a war come the memorials—
tanks, cutlasses, men with cigars.
If women are there they adore
and are saved, shielding their children.

For a long time people rehearse
just how it happened, and you have to learn
how important all that armament was—
and it really could happen again.

So the women and children can wait, whatever
their importance might have been, and they
come to stand around the memorials
and listen some more and be grateful, and smell the cigars.

Then, if your side has won, they explain
how the system works and if you just let it
go on it will prevail everywhere.
And they establish foundations and give
    some of the money back.

Distractions

Think about Gypsies—
like smoke in the evening they cross a border.
They don't believe in it, and they say if God
doesn't care nobody cares. In the morning
their wagons are gone, carrying their stories
away. They like the sound of a wheel
and have given up owning a place. They roll
beyond old newspapers and broken glass and
start a new campfire. Sometimes, going up
a steep hill, they get off and walk forward
and whisper the oldest secret in the world
into the ears of their horses.

In the All-Verbs Navaho World

"The Navaho world is made of verbs."

Left-alone grow-things wait, rustle-grass, click-
trunk, whisper-leaf. You go-people miss the hold-still
dawn, arch-over sky, the jump-everywhere glances.
This woman world, fall-into eyes, reaches out her
makes-tremble beauty, trolls with her body, her
move-everything walk. All-now, our breathe-always
life extends, extends. Change. Change your live-here,
tick-tock hours. Catch all the flit-flit birds,
eat the offer-food, ride over clop-clop land,
our great holds-us-up, wear-a-crown kingdom.

Malheur before Dawn

An owl sound wandered along the road with me.
I didn't hear it—I breathed it into my ears.

Little ones at first, the stars retired, leaving
polished little circles on the sky for awhile.

Then the sun began to shout from below the horizon.
Throngs of birds campaigned, their music a tent of sound.

From across a pond, out of the mist,
one drake made a V and said its name.

Some vast animal of air began to rouse
from the reeds and lean outward.

Frogs discovered their national anthem again.
I didn't know a ditch could hold so much joy.

So magic a time it was that I was both brave and afraid.
Some day like this might save the world.

For Our Party Last Night

It was necessary at the time that the sun
go down—veiled, orange, perfect—
just a touch on the far hills, and that a half moon
hang at a silver height. It was all necessary.
Then where we sat we discussed the news
about art, should it be free. Should our country
support even what shocked some reluctant
people who had to pay. By then in the dusk
fireflies came out. The far hills, mounds of trees,
moved nearer. A lawyer said, "Let the artist paint
but the state needn't pay at all." An artist
said, "But without a living what does freedom mean?"
And by then the stars had spread in a great
arc. At our table where a candle burned
our faces gathered on that little center of light,
while the dark leaned in, large and cool and necessary.

Watching Sandhill Cranes

Spirits among us have departed—friends,
relatives, neighbors: we can't find them.
If we search and call, the sky merely waits.
Then some day here come the cranes
planing in from cloud or mist—sharp,
lonely spears, awkwardly graceful.
They reach for the land; they stalk
the ploughed fields, not letting us near,
not quite our own, not quite the world's.

People go by and pull over to watch. They
peer and point and wonder. It is because
these travelers, these far wanderers,
plane down and yearn in a reaching
flight. They extend our life,
piercing through space to reappear
quietly, undeniably, where we are.

Freedom of Expression

My feet wait there listening, and when
they dislike what happens they begin
to press on the floor. They know when
it is time to walk out on a program. Pretty soon
they are moving, and as the program fades
you can hear the sound of my feet on gravel.

If you have feet with standards, you too
may be reminded—you need not
accept what's given. You gamblers,
pimps, braggarts, oppressive people:—
"Not here," my feet are saying, "no thanks;
let me out of this." And I'm gone.

Cottonwood

By June or July the river flows lazily
shallow and clear among sandbar islands,
and I wade it, zigzag, exploring upstream
where tracks of raccoon, possum, and waterbirds
form a design to be read. Over it all
from millions of saplings that stretch on north,
deep and immense, there arches the odor of cottonwood.

That certain tang in the air, maybe it wrapped
and protected Crazy Horse; it hovered over his blood
when they killed him. It freshened the laundry spread out
in groves where mothers hung washing for wagon trains.
It hovered The West, reminding in the new church,
or jail or tavern, that a great sweep of air waited
beyond, outside, in long curves of the river.

Every breeze brings that pungent but delicate smell.
Embracing the day, I carry it homeward
on hands and clothes, not knowing how sacred
these days: twelve years old, June, July, cottonwood.

Influential Writers

Some of them write too loud.

Some write the mauve poem
    over and over.

In our time a whole tribe have
    campaigned with noisy boots on—
    they look swashbuckling but
    all the syllables finally run and hide.

Their swagger makes them feel good,
    but mobilizes opposition.

Listen—after a torrent begins even big rocks
    have to get out of the way,
    but at the top of the divide you can change
    Mississippi to Columbia with one finger,
    and I did.

But I didn't want the Pacific this big.

Is This Feeling about the West Real?

All their lives out here some people know
they live in a hemisphere beyond what Columbus discovered.
These people look out and wonder: Is it magic? Is it
the oceans of air off the Pacific? You can't
walk through it without wrapping a new
piece of time around you, a readiness for a meadowlark,
that brinkmanship a dawn can carry for lucky people
all through the day.

But if you don't get it, this bonus, you can
go home full of denial, and live out your years.
Great waves can pass unnoticed outside your door;
stars can pound silently on the roof; your teakettle

and cozy life inside can deny everything outside—
whole mountain ranges, history, the holocaust,
sainthood, Crazy Horse.

Listen—something else hovers out here, not
color, not outlines or depth when air
relieves distance by hazing far mountains,
but some total feeling or other world
almost coming forward, like when a bell sounds
and then leaves a whole countryside waiting.

What Gets Away

Little things hide. Sometimes they
scuttle away like dry leaves in a sudden
wind. Tidepools are full of these
panicky creatures, and rock slides
have jittery populations hidden from the world
and even from each other.

Herodotus tells about the shyest
animal there is. It's the one even
Alexander the Great and his whole
conquering army had never seen, and people
—no matter how hard they try—
will never see.

Selections from other volumes (1980-1993)

Why the Sun Comes Up

To be ready again if they find an owl, crows
choose any old tree before dawn and hold a convention
where they practice their outrage routine. "Let's elect
someone." "No, no! Forget it." They
see how many crows can dance on a limb.
"Hey, listen to this one." One old crow
flaps away off and looks toward the east. In that
lonely blackness God begins to speak
in a silence beyond all that moves. Delighted
wings move close and almost touch each other.
Everything stops for a minute, and the sun rises.

Through the Junipers

In the afternoon I wander away through
the junipers. They scatter on low hills
that open and close around me.
If I go far enough, all sight or sound
of people ends. I sit and look endless miles
over waves of those hills.

And then between sentences later when anyone
asks me questions troubling to truth,
my answers wander away and look back.
There are these days, and there are these hills
nobody thinks about, even in summer.
And part of my life doesn't have any home.

Address to the Senior Class

Coming down the hill into this town
I tried to hold in mind the worth of your lives,
to be able to help when Main Street isn't enough any more:
what of the silent storm that is happening now
inside you, the minutes adding to days, and the days
to years, and the time coming when you will lean
for the air that was rich, for the sunbeam, for the sound
going away? I stopped by the roadside to raise
a handful of dust, as the Indians did, to pour it
slowly out and let it fall in a cloud
and the grains tumble together. "This is today,"
I sang. I sang for you till the sun went down.

Notice What This Poem Is Not Doing

The light along the hills in the morning
comes down slowly, naming the trees
white, then coasting the ground for stones to nominate.

Notice what this poem is not doing.

A house, a house, a barn, the old
quarry, where the river shrugs—
how much of this place is yours?

Notice what this poem is not doing.

Every person gone has taken a stone
to hold, and catch the sun. The carving
says, "Not here, but called away."

Notice what this poem is not doing.

The sun, the earth, the sky, all wait.
The crows and redbirds talk. The light
along the hills has come, has found you.

Notice what this poem has not done.

Learning, Any Time

We were singing one day about justice
and a piece of iron fell somewhere
down the street—at least I think
it was justice: it was iron all right.

One time we were early for the rainbow. Lightning
waited, crawling for a place to go.
It would decide in a minute, and then
forget in the gray cloud and maybe stay home.

It is hard to learn that zigzag before
it happens, and not much use after
it's gone—you hold your head still and wonder
about the world: you can't catch it,
    no matter how far or wide or hard.

Strange how things in the world go together
even when you don't try, how music
permeates metal, how a burden you carry
takes on a color or leads to a dream
    you are going to have when the burden is gone.

Learning, they call it, this anticipated
lightning, this thinking around an event
and bringing it right. It is hard to tell
if the connection is yours, or the world's—
    it all comes together and you say, "I know."

But the biggest things and the smallest keep right on.
What's the difference if you understand?—
the heavy will keep on being heavy, and the things
that will get you will get you just the same.

It Still Happens Now

You make me walk my town, its terrible
streets that peel day after day for years
and fall into the sky, till I'm drowned
in time. Even if I shut my eyes the lilacs
come their tide, and Pauline's old house
honks by in a long, low, dying moan
as I fade for my life, wild for this safety
of now, far from the thousand hurts—
those friends moving there still,
fresh, open faces, long bodies leaning
after my last goodby, when war came, and
we left all that seething, and put the lid on.

Key of C—An Interlude for Marvin

Sometime nothing has happened. We are home
at the beginning of summer. Somebody begins
to breathe chords on a harmonica.
"Why don't we tell how our lives will be?"
Sarah says—"I'll start: when I finish
college I'll move East and work in
a bank. In a robbery there a stray bullet
will kill me." Tom quits playing the harmonica:
"I'll work in Dad's drugstore. My wife and child
will die in a fire when the child is three."
He goes on breathing slow notes. Mary
leans back in the porch swing: "I'll marry Tom
and oh I'll hold the little one so close."
"I see exactly," Steve says: "After The War
I'll come back here and you'll all be gone. I don't
want to tell the rest." They turn to me:
"I'll live carefully, and a long time.
Years from now when I'm writing to a friend
I'll tell him what we said today
and how it all came true."—And, oh Marvin,
even this part I'm telling you.

Before It Burned Over: A Sioux Grass Chant

World carpet, robe, every leaf
to look at, brought forth by
buffalo, green places maker, our
own ocean, mother of bodies and
receiver of them, arriving long ago
beginning from wind, seeker
like water of whatever touches
back, aware of stars even after
daylight or blind under snow, far
blanket, bed when we sleep, or in
that long sleep when we become
waving selves, brothers, sisters,
marching together all over the world.

Objector

In line at lunch I cross my fork and spoon
to ward off complicity—the ordered life
our leaders have offered us. Thin as a knife,
our chance to live depends on such a sign
while others talk and The Pentagon from the moon
is bouncing exact commands: "Forget your faith;
be ready for whatever it takes to win: we face
annihilation unless all citizens get in line."

I bow and cross my fork and spoon: somewhere
other citizens more fearfully bow
in a place terrorized by their kind of oppressive state.
Our signs both mean, "You hostages over there
will never be slaughtered by my act." Our vows
cross: never to kill and call it fate.

Living on the Plains [1990]

That winter when this thought came—how the river
held still every midnight and flowed
backward a minute—we studied algebra
late in our room fixed up in the barn,
and I would feel the curved relation,
the rafters upside down, and the cows in their life
holding the earth round and ready
to meet itself again when morning came.

At breakfast while my mother stirred the cereal
she said, "You're studying too hard,"
and I would include her face and hands in my glance
and then look past my father's gaze as
he told again our great race through the stars
and how the world can't keep up with our dreams.

American Gothic

If we see better through tiny,
grim glasses, we like to wear
tiny, grim glasses.
Our parents willed us this
view. It's tundra? We love it.

We travel our kind of
Renaissance: barnfuls of hay,
whole voyages of corn, and
a book that flickers its
halo in the parlor.

Poverty plus confidence equals
pioneers. We never doubted.

Biography

Two days were walking down the street,
one bright, one dark, and both my birthday,
glowing for my head. (Dark is delight for
me. Both my parents are dead.) That street
was the one we lived on, years ago—that is,
    while they lived.

Two days left that place; after my birth
nobody saw two days together ever again,
my mother said; and my father said the same,
but they always liked both kinds and welcomed
dark and light; both glowed for their head,
    while they lived.

The house they knew has opened;
it stands at large in the hills; its
door is the rain; its window, evening.
Today I bend for roof, have shelter
when it's cold, but that great house
arches for all, everywhere, for them, too,
    while I live.

For My Young Friends Who Are Afraid

There is a country to cross you will
find in the corner of your eye, in
the quick slip of your foot—air far
down, a snap that might have caught.
And maybe for you, for me, a high, passing
voice that finds its way by being
afraid. That country is there, for us,
carried as it is crossed. What you fear
will not go away: it will take you into
yourself and bless you and keep you.
That's the world, and we all live there.

Over the Mountains

Maybe someone stumbles across that child
lost weeks ago, now chilled and unconscious but breathing.
Maybe a friendly wanderer saved the child
for awhile, but had to go on, and this is the end.

(The world we all came from reaches out; its trees
embrace; its rocks come down ready to cover
us again. Moss clings to the feet and climbs
carefully, protecting its own. It wants us back.)

Now people carry the child, warm him;
"Save him," they say. Then he stirs and opens his eyes.
He doesn't want what he sees. He closes his eyes.
The slow tide of the forest takes him away.

(This doesn't happen just once; it happens again and again,
to the lost, to searchers and parents, to you, to me.)

How These Words Happened

FROM *A Glass Face in the Rain* (1982)

How It Began

They struggled their legs and blindly loved, those puppies
inside my jacket as I walked through town. They crawled
for warmth and licked each other—their poor mother
dead, and one kind boy to save them. I spread
my arms over their world and hurried along.

At Ellen's place I knocked and waited—the tumult
invading my sleeves, all my jacket alive.
When she came to the door we tumbled—black, white,
gray, hungry—all over the living room floor
together, rolling, whining, happy and blind.

Tuned In Late One Night

Listen—this is a faint station
left alive in the vast universe.
I was left here to tell you a message
designed for your instruction or comfort,
but now that my world is gone I crave
expression pure as all the space
around me: I want to tell what is. . . .

Remember?—we learned that still-face way,
to wait in election or meeting and then
to choose the side that wins, a leader
that lasted, a president that stayed in?
But some of us knew even then it was better
to lose if that was the way our chosen
side came out, in truth, at the end.

It's like this, truth is: it's looking out while everything
happens; being in a place of your own,
between your ears; and any person

you face will get the full encounter
of your self. When you hear any news
you ought to register delight or pain
depending on where you really live.

Now I am fading, with this ambition:
to read with my brights full on,
to write on a clear glass typewriter,
to listen with sympathy,
to speak like a child.

Friends

How far friends are! They forget you,
most days. They have to, I know; but still,
it's lonely just being far and a friend.
I put my hand out—this chair, this table—
so near: touch, that's how to live.
Call up a friend? All right, but the phone
itself is what loves you, warm on your ear,
on your hand. Or, you lift a pen
to write—it's not that far person
but this familiar pen that comforts.
Near things: Friend, here's my hand.

Looking across the River

We were driving the river road.
It was at night. "There's the island,"
someone said. And we all looked across
at the light where the hermit lived.

"I'd be afraid to live there"—
it was Ken the driver who spoke.
He shivered and let us feel
the fear that made him shake.

Over to that dark island
my thought had already crossed—
I felt the side of the house
and the night wind unwilling to rest.

For the first time in all my life
I became someone else:
it was dark; others were going their way;
the river and I kept ours.

We came on home that night;
the road led us on. Everything
we said was louder—it was hollow,
and sounded dark like a bridge.

Somewhere I had lost someone—
so dear or so great or so fine
that I never cared again: as if
time dimmed, and color and sound were gone.

Come for me now, World—
whatever is near, come close.
I have been over the water
and lived there all alone.

Our Cave

Because it was good, we were afraid.
It went down dark, dark. After a
bend it was night. We didn't tell
anybody. All summer it was ours.
I remember best when horses went by
shaking the ground. It was war, we said,
and they wouldn't find us. Once we heard
someone stumbling and crying: we blew out

the candle and waited a long time till quiet.
It came, and the dark was closer than ever.
Now when we close our eyes, we are there
again, anywhere: we hid it well.
We buried in it the best things we had
and covered it over with branches and leaves.

Not Very Loud

Now is the time of the moths that come
in the evening. They are around, just being
there, at windows and doors. They crowd
the lights, planing in from dark fields
and liking it in town. They accept each other
as they fly or crawl. How do they know
what is coming? Their furred flight,
softer than down, announces a quiet
approach under whatever is loud.

What are moths good for? Maybe they offer
something we need, a fluttering
near the edge of our sight, and they may carry
whatever is needed for us to watch
all through those long nights in our still,
vacant houses, if there is another war.

Maybe

Maybe (it's a fear), maybe
someone decides. Maybe it takes
only one. Maybe the end begins.
Maybe it has begun.

It runs through the stages fast,
and they all respond well
and it's over. Then an explorer
comes.

What could they have done?
They could have tried harder.
They could have become meaner.
But maybe nothing—*it happened.*

The explorer turns over a stone.
Maybe those who sang
were the lucky ones.

How It Is

It is war. They put us on a train and
say, "Go." A bell wakes up the engine
as we move along past the crowd,
and a child—one clear small gaze from all the town—
finds my face. I wave. For long I look
back. "I'm not a soldier," I want to say.
But the gaze is left behind. And I'm gone.

In a Corner

Walls hold each other up when they meet;
a ceiling joins them: that corner you can
study, in jail or hospital or school.
I leaned in a corner once when someone
was dying, and I didn't care if the rest
of the walls went anywhere, or if the ceiling
or floor, or if anything—I didn't care.

Now if I'm traveling maybe a bad headache
sends me to lean in a corner. Each eye
has a wall. Father, Mother—they're gone,
and that person died, when I leaned before.
The corner never feels little enough,
and I roll my head for the world, for its need
and this wild, snuggling need and pain of my own.

Remembering

When there was air, when you could
breathe any day if you liked, and if you
wanted to you could run, I used to
climb those hills back of town and
follow a gully so my eyes were at ground
level and could look out through grass as the stems
bent in their tensile way, and see snow
mountains follow along, the way distance goes.

Now I carry those days in a tiny box
wherever I go. I open the lid like this
and let the light glimpse and then glance away.
There is a sigh like my breath when I do this.
Some days I do this again and again.

A Glass Face in the Rain

Sometime you'll walk all night. You'll
come where the sky bends down. You'll turn
aside at a fold in the earth and
be gone from the day.

When the sky turns light again
the land will stare blank for miles
at itself. You won't be there
to see any more.

Back where you lived, for those
who remember well, there will come
a glass face, invisible but still and real,
all night outside in the rain.

Yellow Cars

Some of the cars are yellow, that go
by. Those you look at, so glimmering
when light glances at their passing. Think
of that hope: "Someone will
like me, maybe." The tan ones
don't care, the blue have made
a mistake, the white haven't tried.
But the yellow—you turn your head:
hope lasts a long time if you're happy.

My Life

In my cradle and then driving
my little car, I wave and listen.
(Meanwhile the Cossacks line up together
beyond the horizon, each of them like me,
but maybe older, but lost. But coming.)

Pretty soon I am running. It is
daylight pretty soon and then very bright
across fields by the road. Someone
begins calling. I think it is a person, but maybe
an animal, maybe a bird. I can't tell.

And now it is hard to remember what didn't happen—
did I hear thunder? I stop and look
at the others—does the lightning come
before or after? And even if I find out—
will my soul be happy, out here alone?

From over there in the trees a slant
glance comes, like my father's to find
my mother's, and this film we are in
spins backward, and then I am gone
and pretty soon there isn't any world.

A Message from Space

Everything that happens is the message:
you read an event and be one and wait,
like breasting a wave, all the while knowing
by living, though not knowing how to live.

Or workers build an antenna—a dish
aimed at stars—and they themselves are its message,
crawling in and out, being worlds that loom,
dot-dash, and sirens, and sustaining beams.

And sometimes no one is calling but we turn up
eye and ear—suddenly we fall into
sound before it begins, the breathing
so still it waits there under the breath—

And then the green of leaves calls out, hills
where they wait or turn, clouds in their frenzied
stillness unfolding their careful words:
"Everything counts. The message is the world."

After Arguing against the Contention That Art Must Come from Discontent

Whispering to each handhold, "I'll be back,"
I go up the cliff in the dark. One place
I loosen a rock and listen a long time
till it hits, faint in the gulf, but the rush
of the torrent almost drowns it out, and the wind—
I almost forgot the wind: it tears at your side
or it waits and then buffets; you sag outward. . . .

I remember they said it would be hard. I scramble
by luck into a little pocket out of
the wind and begin to beat on the stones
with my scratched numb hands, rocking back and forth

in silent laughter there in the dark—
"Made it again!" Oh how I love this climb!
—the whispering to stones, the drag, the weight
as your muscles crack and ease on, working
right. They are back there, discontent,
waiting to be driven forth. I pound
on the earth, riding the earth past the stars:
"Made it again! Made it again!"

A Course in Creative Writing

They want a wilderness with a map—
but how about errors that give a new start?—
or leaves that are edging into the light?—
or the many places a road can't find?

Maybe there's a land where you have to sing
to explain anything: you blow a little whistle
just right and the next tree you meet is itself.
(And many a tree is not there yet.)

Things come toward you when you walk.
You go along singing a song that says
where you are going becomes its own
because you start. You blow a little whistle—

And a world begins under the map.

Things I Learned Last Week

Ants, when they meet each other,
usually pass on the right.

Sometimes you can open a sticky
door with your elbow.

A man in Boston has dedicated himself
to telling about injustice.
For three thousand dollars he will
come to your town and tell you about it.

Schopenhauer was a pessimist but
he played the flute.

Yeats, Pound, and Eliot saw art as
growing from other art. They studied that.

If I ever die, I'd like it to be
in the evening. That way, I'll have
all the dark to go with me, and no one
will see how I begin to hobble along.

In The Pentagon one person's job is to
take pins out of towns, hills, and fields,
and then save the pins for later.

Incident

They had this cloud they kept like a zeppelin
tethered to a smokestack, and you couldn't see it
but it sent out these strange little rays
and after a while you felt funny. They had this
man with a box. He pointed it at
the zeppelin and it said, "Jesus!" The man
hurried farther away and called out,
"Hear ye, hear ye!" Then they coaxed
the zeppelin down into the smokestack
and they said, "We won't do that any more."
For a long time the box kept shaking its head,
but it finally said, "OK, forget it." But, quietly,
to us, it whispered, "Let's get out of here."

Fiction

We would get a map of our farm as big
as our farm, and unroll the heavy paper
over the fields, with encouraging things
written here and there—"tomatoes," "corn,"
"creek." Then in the morning we would
stick our heads through and sing, "Barn, be cleaned."
"Plow, turn over the south forty!"
But while our words were going out
on the paper, here would come rumpling
along under the map Old Barney,
just on the ground—he couldn't even
read—going out to slop the hogs.

Our Kind

Our mother knew our worth—
not much. To her, success
was not being noticed at all.
"If we can stay out of jail,"
she said, "God will be proud of us."

"Not worth a row of pins,"
she said, when we looked at the album:
"Grandpa?—ridiculous."
Her hearing was bad, and that
was good: "None of us ever says much."

She sent us forth equipped
for our kind of world, a world of
our betters, in a nation so strong
its greatest claim is no boast,
its leaders telling us all, "Be proud"—

But over their shoulders, God and
our mother, signaling: "Ridiculous."

A Catechism

Who challenged my soldier mother?
    Nobody.
Who kept house for her and fended off the world?
    My father.
Who suffered most from her oppressions?
    My sister.
Who went out into the world to right its wrongs?
    My sister.
Who became bitter when the world didn't listen?
    My sister.
Who challenged my soldier sister?
    Nobody.
Who grew up and saw all this and recorded it and
kept wondering how to solve it but couldn't?
    Guess who.

School Days

1
After the test they sent an expert
questioner to our school: "Who is this
kid Bohr?" When Bohr came in
he asked the expert, "Who are you?"
and for a long time they looked at each other,
and Bohr said, "Thanks, I thought so." Then
they talked about why the test was given.
Afterwards they shook hands, and Bohr walked
slowly away. He turned and called out, "You passed."

2
Enough sleet had pasted over the window
by three o'clock so we couldn't tell if it was dark—
and our pony would be out there in the little shed
waiting to take us home. Teacher banked the stove
with an extra log. That was the storm
of 1934. For two days we waited,

singing and praying, and I guess it worked,
even though the snow drifted over the roof.
But the pony was dead when they dug us out.

3
At a tiny desk inside my desk, a doll
bends over a book. In the book is a feather
found at the beach, from a dead gull.
While Miss Leonard reads "The Highwayman,"
I bend over my book and cry,
and fly all alone through the night
toward being the person I am.

We Interrupt to Bring You

It will be coming toward Earth, and
a cameraman who happens to be on Mt. Palomar or
somewhere will catch it, live, for the news,
and I'll be going to the bathroom or something
and miss it; or maybe I'm out raking leaves
in the yard, or it's one of those days I'm home
with flu, and being feverish I doze, but it's
all right to skip work because I'm really
sick, a little bit; anyway, it's the greatest
scene ever, and I don't see it—they call
an alert, and everybody panics; it's coming
like mad, and everybody hightails out—
they clear New York, and all the people rush
into shelters or those new domes on the ocean
floor, and everybody's gone, and the domes
collapse, and I'm the only one left.

And it's still coming on toward Earth, but
at the last minute it misses, and I
come back from the bathroom or from raking,
or just wake up, and the channels are funny;
I switch around and find one still going—it's
on automatic pilot or something—and it just

keeps going back and back through old commercials
and Saturday morning horrors, and people are all
dead, or gone anyway, but the world is
saved and I'm watching this one dim channel,
thinking: it's still a good day even though
I can't get Perry Mason—the leaves
are all raked, and I'm not very sick, really.

My Mother Was a Soldier

If no one moved on order, she would kill—
that's what the gun meant, soldier. No one
told you? Her eye went down the barrel; her hand
held still; gunpowder paid all that it owed
at once. No need to count the dead.

Hunting, she dragged the bait till nightfall, then
hung it in a tree and waited. Time
was working for her, and the quiet. What a world
it is, for thinkers! Contact would come, and
the wildest foe fall fastest, Mother said.

Tapping on my wrist, she talked: "Patience
is the doctor; it says try; it says
they think we're nice, we quiet ones, we die
so well: that's how we win, imagining things
before they happen." "No harm in being quiet,"

My mother said: "that's the sound that finally wins."

When You Go Anywhere

This passport your face (not you
officially, your picture, but the face
used to make the passport) offers
everyone its witness: "This is me."

It feels like only a picture, a passport
forced upon you. Somewhere this oval,
sudden and lasting, appeared. It happened
that you were behind it, like it or not.

You present it—your passport, your face—
wherever you go. It says, "A little country,"
it says, "Allow this observer
quiet passage," it says, "Ordinary," it says, "Please."

Once in the 40s

We were alone one night on a long
road in Montana. This was in winter, a big
night, far to the stars. We had hitched,
my wife and I, and left our ride at
a crossing to go on. Tired and cold—but
brave—we trudged along. This, we said,
was our life, watched over, allowed to go
where we wanted. We said we'd come back some time
when we got rich. We'd leave the others and find
a night like this, whatever we had to give,
and no matter how far, to be so happy again.

Around You, Your House

I give you the rain, its long hollow
room all the way down to the streetlight
yellow under midnight. I give you the sound
you can hear when drops are talking to
themselves while you are staring from a window.
I give you a letter. You can fold it again
and carry it when you walk back to the fire
where you stand for a while. I give you the poker
for stirring what burns, one page at a time.
The last flames up the draft and out
into the night, and I give you the rain.

Ruby Was Her Name

My mother, who opened my eyes, who
brought me into the terrible world,
was guilty. Her look apologized:
she knew what anyone said was true about us
but therefore unfair. How could they blame us
for doing the things we were set to do?

Never heroic, never a model
for us, or for anyone, she cowered
and looked from the corner of her eye—
"Et tu?" And it always meant we were
with her, alas. No one else
could find the center of the world.

She found the truth like a victim; it hit
her again and again, and she always cried out.
At the end she turned to me, helplessly
honest still: "Oh, Bill, I'm afraid,"
and the whole of her life went back to her heart,
from me in a look for the look she gave.

Letting You Go

Day brings what is going to be. Trees—
wherever they are—begin to stand.
I have a crossing to do today
onward through this shadowy land.

How still earth stayed that night at first
when you didn't breathe. I couldn't believe
how carefully moonlight came. It was
like the time by my mother's grave.

Today I am going on. In former times
when you were back there, then

I tried to hold the moon and sun.
Now when they ask me who you were—

I remember, but remember my promise.
And I say, "No one."

Troubleshooting

On still days when country telephone
wires go south, go home, go quietly away into
the woods, a certain little brown bird appears,
hopping and flying by starts, following the line,
trying out each pole.
My father and I, troubleshooting for the telephone
company back then, used to see that same bird
along old roads, and it led us to farms
we always thought about owning some day.

When I see that bird now I see my father
tilt his hat and flip the pliers confidently
into the toolbox; the noise of my life, and all
the buffeting from those who judge and pass by,
dwindle off and sink into the silence,
and the little brown bird steadfastly wanders on
pulling what counts wherever it goes.

Remembering Brother Bob

Tell me, you years I had for my life,
tell me a day, that day it snowed
and I played hockey in the cold.
Bob was seven, then, and I was twelve,

and strong. The sun went down. I turned
and Bob was crying on the shore.

Do I remember kindness? Did I
shield my brother, comfort him?
Tell me, you years I had for my life.

Yes, I carried him. I took
him home. But I complained. I see
the darkness; it comes near: and Bob,
who is gone now, and the other kids.
I am the zero in the scene:
"You said you would be brave," I chided
him. "I'll not take you again."
Years, I look at the white across
this page, and think: I never did.

Places with Meaning

Say it's a picnic on the Fourth of July
and all of those usual at the end of day are there.
While they look at each other they become old,
and from the dark wood of evening a heron
rows forward across the path of sky left
in the west, through the still air.

All of my life I have noticed these appropriate landscapes
where events find their equivalent forms: oftentimes
I see trees hunching their shoulders, leaning toward me,
because in the past I have neglected what I should have done;
or a dog hurries forward to lick some hands, and all
at once I see how frightening: they are mine.

There are people who always belong wherever Earth brings
them and gives them over to the practices of the wind;
more slowly, but caught in the same pressure, the rest of us
too, by the end of our days, learn to lean forward
out of our lives to find that what passes has molded
everything we touch or see, outside or in.

With Neighbors One Afternoon

Someone said, stirring their tea, "I would
come home any time just for this,
to look out the clear backyard air
and then into the cup."

You could see the tiniest pattern of bark on the trees
and every slight angle of color change
in the sunshine—millions of miles of gold light
lavished on people like us.

You could put out your hand and feel the rush of years
rounding your life into these days of ours.
From somewhere a leaf came gliding slowly down
and rested on the lawn.

Remember that scene?—inside it you folded the last
of your jealousy and hate, and all those deeds so hard
to forget. Absolution: swish!—you took
the past into your mouth,

And swallowed it, warm, thin, bitter, and good.

A Journey

Through many doors it's been—through
that first into light, afraid, crying
for fear, for air, no going back.
Then other doors: the one where shadows
waited like night, the one nobody
opened when I knocked, and the one where somebody
did. (It was over a cliff and I fell.)

One time there wasn't any door; I turned to look
where I had been—only that? Only
those meaningless windows leading down one
by one to the faint small beginning?

Past the middle of life, and nothing
done—but a voice came on: "I am
the door," someone said. I closed my eyes;
whatever I touched led on.

Friends, Farewell

After the chores are done I tune
and strum. Nobody hears, nobody cares,
and the stars go on.

Now that I've told you this, maybe
I've been all wrong—so faint a life,
and so little done.

But I want you all to be easy after
I'm gone: nobody hear, nobody care,
and the stars go on.

If I Could Be Like Wallace Stevens

The octopus would be my model—
it wants to understand; it prowls
the rocks a hundred ways and holds
its head aloof but not ignoring.
All its fingers value what
they find. "I'd rather know," they say,
"I'd rather slime along than be heroic."

My pride would be to find out; I'd
bow to see, play the fool,
ask, beg, retreat like a wave—
but somewhere deep I'd hold the pearl,
never tell. "Mr. Charley,"
I'd say, "talk some more. Boast again."
And I'd play the banjo and sing.

Salvaged Parts

Fire took the house. Black bricks
tell how it went. Wild roses
try to say it never happened.

A rock my foot pushed falls
for years down the cellar stairs. . . .
No thanks, no home again for me—

Mine burned before it burned.
A rose pretends, but I always knew:
a rose pretends, a rock tells how it is.

One Time

When evening had flowed between houses
and paused on the schoolground, I met
Hilary's blind little sister following
the gray smooth railing still warm from the sun
with her hand; and she stood by the edge
holding her face upward waiting
while the last light found her cheek
and her hair, and then on over the trees.

You could hear the great sprinkler arm
of water find and then leave the pavement,
and pigeons telling each other their dreams
or the dreams they would have. We were
deep in the well of shadow by then, and I
held out my hand, saying, "Tina, it's me—
Hilary says I should tell you it's dark,
and, oh, Tina, it is. Together now—"

And I reached, our hands touched,
and we found our way home.

Pegleg Lookout

Those days, having the morning clouds, and with no one
around, it was quiet on the lookout.
For breakfast I ate animal crackers
and milk in a blue bowl marked
"World's Fair, 1939." Some of the figures
looked like my mother. I saved those till last.
Then I sat on the deck reading *War
and Peace, The Magic Mountain, David
Copperfield*—the big ones I'd brought. Four times
an hour I paced the catwalk to look
for smokes—nothing, the miles of pine tops
and then Mount Shasta. Those days I ate
the whole world, lined up my books and animals,
slowly erased all the trials and insults
the times had brought. I balanced my life
there a whole year. One day I washed
the blue bowl the last time and came down again.

FROM *An Oregon Message* (1987)

Keeping a Journal

At night it was easy for me with my little candle
to sit late recording what happened that day. Sometimes
rain breathing in from the dark would begin softly
across the roof and then drum wildly for attention.
The candle flame would hunger after each wafting
of air. My pen inscribed thin shadows that leaned
forward and hurried their lines along the wall.

More important than what was recorded, these evenings
deepened my life: they framed every event
or thought and placed it with care by the others.
As time went on, that scribbled wall—even if
it stayed blank—became where everything
recognized itself and passed into meaning.

First Grade

In the play Amy didn't want to be
anybody; so she managed the curtain.
Sharon wanted to be Amy. But Sam
wouldn't let anybody be anybody else—
he said it was wrong. "All right," Steve said,
"I'll be me, but I don't like it."
So Amy was Amy, and we didn't have the play.
And Sharon cried.

A Life, a Ritual

My mother had a child, one dark
like her, but bland—wide gaze—who stared
where eternity was, then back to her eyes,
and the world. A blanket protected, a song
instructed, and the years came along, came along.

There are people whose game is success, but others
hear distance: guided, often betrayed,
they wander their lives. Their voices go by
every day, outside of history, outside
of importance. They ritual whatever they do.

My mother is nothing now. Her child—
wide gaze like hers—remembers the blanket,
and the song that taught how to lose. Oh, shadow
that came large on a wall, then face that recognized
mine: this distant song about failure

Is for you, is for you.

Surrounded by Mountains

Digging potatoes east of Sapporo
we would listen at noon to world news.

The little radio was in one of the furrows,
propped against a lunch bucket.

We didn't make any judgments. Our fields
were wide, slanting from wooded foothills.

    Religious leaders called for
    a revival of spirit in the world.

    Certain statesmen from important
    nations were considering a summit meeting.

Old Mrs. Osaka, permanently
bent over, stirred the clods beside her.

Rice fields, yellow as sunflowers,
marked off kilometers below us.

The shrine where the crows lived
had a bell that told us when rest was over.

Goodby, old friends. I remember the Prime Minister
talking, and the water jar in the shade.

Little Rooms

I rock high in the oak—secure, big branches—
at home while darkness comes. It gets lonely up here
as lights needle forth below, through airy space.
Tinkling dishwashing noises drift up, and a faint
smooth gush of air through leaves, cool evening
moving out over the earth. Our town leans farther

away, and I ride through the arch toward midnight,
holding on, listening, hearing deep roots grow.

There are rooms in a life, apart from others, rich
with whatever happens, a glimpse of moon, a breeze.
You who come years from now to this brief spell
of nothing that was mine: the open, slow passing
of time was a gift going by. I have put my hand out
on the mane of the wind, like this, to give it to you.

The Big House

She was a modern, you know.
He, you know, dealt in land.
They maintained, you know, several gardens.
You know, when the wind blows, their flowers are famous.

Their house was well built, they say.
And they say the foundation had rock under it.
Some of the walls, they say, were two feet thick.
An artist, they say, designed the door handle.

Construction took I don't know how long,
and I don't know how many bedrooms.
They needed I don't know how big a plan.
But the whole thing—I don't know how—fell down.

They're gone, they say, you know. I don't know where.

Next Time

Next time what I'd do is look at
the earth before saying anything. I'd stop
just before going into a house
and be an emperor for a minute

and listen better to the wind
    or to the air being still.

When anyone talked to me, whether
blame or praise or just passing time,
I'd watch the face, how the mouth
had to work, and see any strain, any
sign of what lifted the voice.

And for all, I'd know more—the earth
bracing itself and soaring, the air
finding every leaf and feather over
forest and water, and for every person
the body glowing inside the clothes
    like a light.

Burning a Book

Protecting each other, right in the center
a few pages glow a long time.
The cover goes first, then outer leaves
curling away, then spine and a scattering.
Truth, brittle and faint, burns easily,
its fire as hot as the fire lies make—
flame doesn't care. You can usually find
a few charred words in the ashes.

And some books ought to burn, trying for character
but just faking it. More disturbing
than book ashes are whole libraries that no one
got around to writing—desolate
towns, miles of unthought-in cities,
and the terrorized countryside where wild dogs
own anything that moves. If a book
isn't written, no one needs to burn it—
ignorance can dance in the absence of fire.

So I've burned books. And there are many
I haven't even written, and nobody has.

Thinking about Being Called Simple by a Critic

I wanted the plums, but I waited.
The sun went down. The fire
went out. With no lights on
I waited. From the night again—
those words: how stupid I was.
And I closed my eyes to listen.
The words all sank down, deep
and rich. I felt their truth
and began to live them. They were mine
to enjoy. Who but a friend
could give so sternly what the sky
feels for everyone but few learn to
cherish? In the dark with the truth
I began the sentence of my life
and found it so simple there was no way
back into qualifying my thoughts
with irony or anything like that.
I went to the fridge and opened it—
sure enough the light was on.
I reached in and got the plums.

Serving with Gideon

Now I remember: in our town the druggist
prescribed Coca-Cola mostly, in tapered
glasses to us, and to the elevator
man in a paper cup, so he could
drink it elsewhere because he was black.

And now I remember The Legion—gambling
in the back room, and no women but girls, old boys
who ran the town. They were generous,
to their sons or the sons of friends.
And of course I was almost one.

I remember winter light closing
its great blue fist slowly eastward

along the street, and the dark then, deep
as war, arched over a radio show
called the thirties in the great old U.S.A.

Look down, stars—I was almost
one of the boys. My mother was folding
her handkerchief; the library seethed and sparked;
right and wrong arced; and carefully
I walked with my cup toward the elevator man.

Ground Zero [December 1982]

A bomb photographed me on the stone,
on a white wall, a burned outline where
the bomb rays found me out in the open
and ended me, person and shadow, never to cast
a shadow again, but be here so light
the sun doesn't know. People on Main Street
used to stand in their certain chosen places—
I walk around them. It wouldn't be right
if I stood there. But all of their shadows are mine now—
I am so white on the stone.

Looking for Gold

A flavor like wild honey begins
when you cross the river. On a sandbar
sunlight stretches out its limbs, or is it
a sycamore, so brazen, so clean and bold?
You forget about gold. You stare—and a flavor
is rising all the time from the trees.
Back from the river, over by a thick
forest, you feel the tide of wild honey
flooding your plans, flooding the hours
till they waver forward looking back. They can't

return: that river divides more than
two sides of your life. The only way
is farther, breathing that country, becoming
wise in its flavor, a native of the sun.

Stillborn

Where a river touches an island
under willows leaning over
I watch the waves and think of you,
    who almost lived.

Stars will rake the sky again,
and time go on, the dark, the cold.
Clouds will race when the wind begins,
    where you almost were.

But while the thunder shakes the world
and the graceful dance and the powerful win,
still faithful, still in thought, I bow,
    little one.

Honeysuckle

Not yet old enough, still only a kid,
you meet Hazel. She is not old enough either—
it is the world before: it is early. The two of you
walk through slow, heavy, thick air.

Now you are coming to the corner where hummingbirds have
their nest. You breathe. It is the honeysuckle
tangled along the church wall. Each of you
takes a blossom to taste as you say goodby.

That flavor lasts a long time. Forever.

School Play

You were a princess, lost; I
was a little bird. Nobody cared
where we went or how we sang.
A storm, I seem to remember, a giant
wave, some kind of crash at the end.
I think we cried when they took off our wings.

If time should happen again—and it could;
we're still in a play, you know—maybe
we'll hide so well the wave will pass
and after the storm we'll come out. We both
will really believe what, even then, we knew:
not the princess, not the bird—but the song—
        was true.

A Ceremony: Doing the Needful

Carrying you, a little model carefully dressed
up, nestled on velvet in a tiny box,
I climb a mountain west of Cody. Often,
cut by snow, sheltering to get warm, I take
you out and prop you on the rocks, looking south
each time. You can see the breaks, down through cedars
to miles of tan grass. I put you back in the box
and hold you inside my coat. At the top I put you
wedged in a line of boulders, out of the wind.
It is very late by now, getting dark. I leave
you there. All the way down I can hear the earth
explaining necessity and how cold it is when you walk
away, even though you've done all you can.

For the Unknown Enemy

This monument is for the unknown
good in our enemies. Like a picture
their life began to appear: they
gathered at home in the evening
and sang. Above their fields they saw
a new sky. A holiday came
and they carried the baby to the park
for a party. Sunlight surrounded them.

Here we glimpse what our minds long turned
away from. The great mutual
blindness darkened that sunlight in the park,
and the sky that was new, and the holidays.
This monument says that one afternoon
we stood here letting a part of our minds
escape. They came back, but different.
Enemy: one day we glimpsed your life.

This monument is for you.

Being an American

Some network has bought history, all the rights
for wars and games. At home the rest of us
wait. Nothing happens, of course.
We know that somewhere our times are
alive and flashing, for real. We sigh.
If we had been rich we could have lived
like that. Maybe even yet we could buy
a little bit of today and see how it is.

Over the North Jetty

Geese and brant, their wingbeat
steady—it's a long flight, Alaska—
bank their approach and then curve
upwind for landing. They live where storms
are so usual they are almost fair weather.

And we lean in that permanent gale,
watching those cold flocks depend on their wings
as they veer out of the north. In the last flight
one laggard pulls farther downwind
and peels off to disappear alone in the storm.

If you follow an individual away like that
a part of your life is lost forever,
beating somewhere in darkness, and belonging
only to storms that haunt around the world
on that risky path just over the wave.

Waiting in Line

You the very old, I have come
to the edge of your country and looked across,
how your eyes warily look into mine
when we pass, how you hesitate when
we approach a door. Sometimes
I understand how steep your hills
are, and your way of seeing the madness
around you, the careless waste of the calendar,
the rush of people on buses. I have
studied how you carry packages,
balancing them better, giving them attention.
I have glimpsed from within the gray-eyed look
at those who push, and occasionally even I
can achieve your beautiful bleak perspective

on the loud, the inattentive, shoving boors
jostling past you toward their doom.

With you, from the pavement I have watched
the nation of the young, like jungle birds
that scream as they pass, or gyrate on playgrounds,
their frenzied bodies jittering with the disease
of youth. Knowledge can cure them. But
not all at once. It will take time.

There have been evenings when the light
has turned everything silver, and like you
I have stopped at a corner and suddenly
staggered with the grace of it all: to have
inherited all this, or even the bereavement
of it and finally being cheated!—the chance
to stand on a corner and tell it goodby!
Every day, every evening, every
abject step or stumble has become heroic:—

You others, we the very old have a country.
A passport costs everything there is.

An Oregon Message

When we first moved here, pulled
the trees in around us, curled
our backs to the wind, no one
had ever hit the moon—no one.
Now our trees are safer than the stars,
and only other people's neglect
is our precious and abiding shell,
pierced by meteors, radar, and the telephone.

From our snug place we shout
religiously for attention, in order to hide:
only silence or evasion will bring
dangerous notice, the hovering hawk

of the state, or the sudden quiet stare
and fatal estimate of an alerted neighbor.

This message we smuggle out in
its plain cover, to be opened
quietly: Friends everywhere—
we are alive! Those moon rockets
have missed millions of secret
places! Best wishes.

Burn this.

Why I Am Happy

Now has come, an easy time. I let it
roll. There is a lake somewhere
so blue and far nobody owns it.
A wind comes by and a willow listens
gracefully.

I hear all this, every summer. I laugh
and cry for every turn of the world,
its terribly cold, innocent spin.
That lake stays blue and free; it goes
on and on.

And I know where it is.

Final Exam: American Renaissance

Fill in blanks: Your name is
_____ ____ldo Emerson. Your friend
Thor_____ lives at _____ Pond; he owes
you rent and an ax. Your
neighbor in a house with _____ gables

won't respond to another neighbor, Herman
_____, who broods about a whale colored _____.
You think it is time for America to _____.

In a few choice words, tell why.

Purifying the Language of the Tribe

Walking away means
"Goodby."

Pointing a knife at your stomach means
"Please don't say that again."

Leaning toward you means
"I love you."

Raising a finger means
"I enthusiastically agree."

"Maybe" means
"No."

"Yes" means
"Maybe."

Looking like this at you means
"You had your chance."

Starting with Little Things

Love the earth like a mole,
fur-near. Nearsighted,
hold close the clods,
their fine-print headlines.
Pat them with soft hands—

But spades, but pink and loving: they
break rock, nudge giants aside,
affable plow.
Fields are to touch:
each day nuzzle your way.

Tomorrow the world.

Ultimate Problems

In the Aztec design God crowds
into the little pea that is rolling
out of the picture.
All the rest extends bleaker
because God has gone away.

In the White Man design, though,
no pea is there.
God is everywhere,
but hard to see.
The Aztecs frown at this.

How do you know He is everywhere?
And how did He get out of the pea?

When I Met My Muse

I glanced at her and took my glasses
off—they were still singing. They buzzed
like a locust on the coffee table and then
ceased. Her voice belled forth, and the
sunlight bent. I felt the ceiling arch, and
knew that nails up there took a new grip
on whatever they touched. "I am your own
way of looking at things," she said. "When
you allow me to live with you, every
glance at the world around you will be
a sort of salvation." And I took her hand.

Ghalib Decides to Be Reticent

There is a question I would like to ask
the world. But I don't think I will ever ask it.

Strange to think—I have thought too far
and now must hide a discovery.

I couldn't make the world, or even change it,
but I can find something here and keep it before I go.

Friends, if you knew what I'm talking about
you would be glad that I didn't tell you.

The Sparkle Depends on Flaws in the Diamond

Wood that can learn is no good for a bow.

The eye that can stand the sun can't
    see in shadow.

Fish don't find the channel—the channel
    finds them.

If the root doesn't trust, the plant
    won't blossom.

A dog that knows jaguars is no longer
    useful in hunting.

You can lie at a banquet, but you have to
    be honest in the kitchen.

Ode to Garlic

Sudden, it comes for you
in the cave of yourself where you know
and are lifted by important events.

Say you are dining and it happens:
soaring like an eagle, you are
pierced by a message from the midst of life:

Memory—what holds the days together—touches
your tongue. It is from deep in the earth
and it reaches out kindly, saying, "Hello, Old Friend."

It makes us alike, all offspring of powerful
forces, part of one great embrace of democracy,
united across every boundary.

You walk out generously, giving it back
in a graceful wave, what you've been given.
Like a child again, you breathe on the world, and it shines.

Turn Over Your Hand

Those lines on your palm, they can be read
for a hidden part of your life that only
those links can say—nobody's voice
can find so tiny a message as comes
across your hand. Forbidden to complain,
you have tried to be like somebody else,
and only this fine record you examine
sometimes like this can remember where
you were going before that long
silent evasion that your life became.

1932

Nobody could come because ours was the house
with the quarantine sign in red, "Scarlet Fever."
We looked out through the tree that whispered all night
its green "Life, life in the world."

Others had school. They would live. They
could run past every day and not look.
At night we listened for stars, and we talked
of miles we would go sometime if our house
let us out, if the doctor ever said yes.

When they took the sign down it was over,
but we carried a lesson the stars had brought,
those times when people turned away.

1940

It is August. Your father is walking you
to the train for camp and then the War
and on out of his life, but you don't know.

Little lights along the path glow under their hoods
and your shoes go brown, brown in the brightness
till the next interval, when they disappear in the shadow.

You know they are down there, by the crunch of stone
and a rustle when they touch a fern. Somewhere above,
cicadas arch their gauze of sound all over town.

Shivers of summer wind follow across the park
and then turn back. You walk on toward
September, the depot, the dark, the light, the dark.

108 East Nineteenth

Mother, the sweet peas have gushed out of
the ground where you fell, where you lay that day
when the doctor came, while your wash kept flapping
on the line across the backyard. I stood
and looked out a long time toward the Fairgrounds.
The Victrola in the living room used to play
"Nola," and the room spun toward a center
that our neighborhood clustered around. Nasturtiums
you put in our salad would brighten our tummies,
you said, and we careened off like trains
to play tag in alfalfa fields till the moon
came out and you called us home with "Popcorn
for all who come." But that was long
before you said, "Jesus is calling me home."

And Father, when your summons came and you quietly
left, no one could hold you
back. You didn't need to talk
because your acts for years had already prayed.
For you both, may God guide my hand in its pious
act, from far off, across this page.

Mother's Day

Peg said, "This one," and we bought it
for Mother, our allowance for weeks
paid out to a clerk who snickered—
a hideous jar, oil-slick in color,
glass that light got lost in.

We saw it for candy, a sign for
our love. And it lasted:
the old house on Eleventh,
a dim room on Crescent where
the railroad shook the curtains,
that brief glory at Aunt Mabel's place.

Peg thought it got more beautiful,
Egyptian, sort of, a fire-sheened
relic. And with a doomed grasp
we carried our level of aesthetics
with us across Kansas, proclaiming
our sentimental badge.

Now Peg says, "Remember that candy jar?"
She smoothes the silver. "Mother
hated it." I am left standing
alone by the counter, ready to buy what
will hold Mother by its magic, so
she will never be mad at us again.

A Memorial for My Mother

For long my life left hers. It went
among strangers; it weakened and followed
foreign ways, even honesty, and courage. It found
those most corrupting of all temptations,
friends—their grace, their faithfulness.

But now my life has come back. In our bleak
little town I taste salt and smoke again.
I turn into our alley and lean
where I hid from work or from anything
deserving of praise. Mother, you and I—

We knew if they knew our hearts they would blame.
We knew we deserved nothing. I go along
now being no one, and remembering this—
how alien we were from others, how hard we chewed
on our town's tough rind. How we loved its flavor.

How It Is with Family

Let's assume you have neglected to write
a brother or a sister. The closeness you had for years
is gone. But now there's a need—let's assume
it's about money or something. You still know
them so well you feel right about it. You begin,
and even if they don't respond, your words and the whole
idea go along as part of the world: you don't have to
be correct. You say, "It's Bob, "It's Peg," "I'm just
writing them." Let's assume someone blames
you—the reaching out as if no time had passed.
You're surprised: there's a part of the way things are
that calculating people can't know. You don't
waste much time following out that strangeness, you
just write, "Bob," or "Peg," "It's me—send the money."

Saint Matthew and All

Lorene—we thought she'd come home. But
it got late, and then days. Now
it has been years. Why shouldn't she,
if she wanted? I would: something comes
along, a sunny day, you start walking;
you meet a person who says, "Follow me,"
and things lead on.

Usually, it wouldn't happen, but sometimes
the neighbors notice your car is gone, the
patch of oil in the driveway, and it fades.
They forget.

In the Bible it happened—fishermen, Levites.
They just went away and kept going. Thomas,
away off in India, never came back.

But Lorene—it was a stranger maybe, and he
said, "Your life, I need it." And nobody else did.

Run before Dawn

Most mornings I get away, slip out
the door before light, set forth on the dim, gray
road, letting my feet find a cadence
that softly carries me on. Nobody
is up—all alone my journey begins.

Some days it's escape: the city is burning
behind me, cars have stalled in their tracks,
and everybody is fleeing like me but some other direction.
My stride is for life, a far place.

Other days it is hunting: maybe some game will cross
my path and my stride will follow for hours, matching
all turns. My breathing has caught the right beat
for endurance; familiar trancelike scenes glide by.

And sometimes it's a dream of motion, streetlights coming near,
passing, shadows that lean before me, lengthened
then fading, and a sound from a tree: a soul, or an owl.

These journeys are quiet. They mark my days with adventure
too precious for anyone else to share, little gems
of darkness, the world going by, and my breath, and the road.

By a River in the Osage Country

They called it Neosho, meaning
"a river made muddy by buffalo."
You don't need many words if you
already know what you're talking about,
and they did. But later there was
nothing they knew that made any difference.

I am thinking of those people—say one
of them looks at you; for an instant you see
a soul like your own, and you are both

lost. What the spirit has given
you to do is unworthy. Two kinds of
dirt, you look at each other.

But still, I have waded that river
and looked into the eyes of buffalo
that were standing and gazing far:
no soul I have met knew the source
that well, or where the Neosho
went when it was clear.

Arrival

While the years were mine I walked the high country
with a thought for a friend: *Somewhere, somewhere.*

And I heard the wind in its desperate quiet
smuggling winter through the dark forest.

I saw leaves massacred in autumn,
and their places taken by the stars at night.

In all the world no place was mine
because I was driven like the other things.

But then I found the tumbleweed secret,
bounding along saying, "Where is my home?"

And the voices began to come at night,
warning, "We're lost—don't be like us."

So when someone is near I reach out for them,
knowing how far it is when you're alone—

How out in space you finally accept
what has to be: *Anywhere, anywhere.*

FROM *Passwords* (1991)

Dedications / Pledges / Commitments

For the past.
For my own path.
For surprises.

For mistakes that worked so well.
For tomorrow if I'm there.
For the next real thing.

Then for carrying it all
through whatever is necessary.
For following the little god who speaks only to me.

Story Time

Tell that one about Catherine
who carried her doll to college
and when her baby died
she threw her doll in the river.
    Tell that one.

And the one when the old engineer
liked his locomotive so much
he lived there and they had to
build him a house with a whistle.
    I like that.

And the successful racehorse with a fancy stall
fixed up like a Western clubhouse
with an old tennis shoe nailed
for luck above the door.
    That's a good one.

But I'm tired of this long story
where I live, these houses with people

who whisper their real lives away
while eternity runs wild in the street,
    and you suffocate.

Yes, and how about the boy who always
granted others their way to live,
and he gave away his whole life
till at last nothing was left for him?
    Don't tell that one.

Bring me a new one, maybe with a dog
that trots alongside, and a desert with a hidden
river no one else finds, but you go there
and pray and a great voice comes.
    And everything listens.

The Way I Write

In the mornings I lie partly propped up
the way Thomas Jefferson did when he slept
at Monticello. Then I stop and
look away like Emily Dickinson when
she was thinking about the carriage and the fly.

When someone disturbs me I come back
like Pascal from those infinite spaces,
but I don't have his great reassurances
of math following along with me; so somehow
the world around me is even scarier.

Besides, the world on fire of Saint Teresa
surrounds me, and the wild faces Dante
awakened on his descent through those dark
forbidden caverns. But over my roof bends
my own kind sky and the mouse-nibble sound of now.

The sky has waited a long time
for this day. Trees have reached out,

the river has scrambled to get where it is.
And here I bring my little mind
to the edge of the ocean and let it think.

My head lolls to one side as thoughts
pour onto the page, important
additions but immediately obsolete, like waves.
The ocean and I have many pebbles
to find and wash off and roll into shape.

"What happens to all these rocks?" "They
become sand." "And then?" My hand stops.
Thomas Jefferson, Emily Dickinson,
Pascal, Dante—they all pause too.
The sky waits. I lean forward and write.

Reading with Little Sister: A Recollection

The stars have died overhead in their great cold.
Beneath us the sled whispers along. Back there
our mother is gone. They tell us, "If you hold on
the dogs will take you home." And they tell us never
to cry. We'll die too, they say, if we
are ever afraid. All night we hold on.
The stars go down. We are never afraid.

The Day Millicent Found the World

Every morning Millicent ventured farther
into the woods. At first she stayed
near light, the edge where bushes grew, where
her way back appeared in glimpses among
dark trunks behind her. Then by farther paths
or openings where giant pines had fallen
she explored ever deeper into
the interior, till one day she stood under a great

dome among columns, the heart of the forest, and knew:
Lost. She had achieved a mysterious world
where any direction would yield only surprise.

And now not only the giant trees were strange
but the ground at her feet had a velvet nearness;
intricate lines on bark wove messages all
around her. Long strokes of golden sunlight
shifted over her feet and hands. She felt
caught up and breathing in a great powerful embrace.
A birdcall wandered forth at leisurely intervals
from an opening on her right: "Come away, Come away."
Never before had she let herself realize
that she was part of the world and that it would follow
wherever she went. She was part of its breath.

Aunt Dolbee called her back that time, a high
voice tapering faintly among the farthest trees,
"Milli-cent! Milli-cent!" And that time she returned,
but slowly, her dress fluttering along pressing
back branches, her feet stirring up the dark smell
of moss, and her face floating forward, a stranger's
face now, with a new depth in it, into the light.

News Every Day

Birds don't say it just once. If they like it
they say it again. And again, every morning.
I heard a bird congratulating itself
all day for being a jay.
Nobody cared. But it was glad
all over again, and said so, again.

Many people are fighting each other, in the world.
You could learn that and say, "Many people
are fighting each other, in the world."
It would be true, but saying it wouldn't
make any difference. But you'd say it.
Birds are like that. People are like that.

An Afternoon in the Stacks

Closing the book, I find I have left my head
inside. It is dark in here, but the chapters open
their beautiful spaces and give a rustling sound,
words adjusting themselves to their meaning.
Long passages open at successive pages. An echo,
continuous from the title onward, hums
behind me. From in here the world looms,
a jungle redeemed by these linked sentences
carved out when an author traveled and a reader
kept the way open. When this book ends
I will pull it inside-out like a sock
and throw it back in the library. But the rumor
of it will haunt all that follows in my life.
A candleflame in Tibet leans when I move.

Paso por Aquí

Comanches tell how the buffalo
wore down their own pass through these hills,
herds pouring over for years, not finding
a way but making it by going there.
Comanche myself, I bow my head
in the graveyard at Buffalo Gap and begin
to know the world as a land invented
by breath, its hills and plains guided
and anchored in place by thought, by feet.

Tombstones lean all around—marble, and pitiful
limestone agonies, recording in worn-out words
the travailed, the loved bodies that rest here.
No one comes quietly enough to surprise them;
the earth brims with whatever they gave. It spills
long horizons ahead of us, and we part its grass
from above, staring hard enough to begin

to see a world, long like Texas,
deep as history goes after it happens,
and ahead of us, pawed by our impatience.

We came over the plains. Where are we going?

Old Blue

Some day I'll crank up that Corvette, let it
mumble those marvelous oil-swimming gears
and speak its authority. I'll rock its big wheels
till they roll free onto the drive. Nobody can
stop us then: loaded with everything, we'll pick up
momentum for the hill north of town. Mona,
you didn't value me and it's too late now.
Steve, remember your refusal to go along on
those deals when you all opposed me?—you had
your chance. Goodby, you squealers and grubbies;
goodby, old house that begins to leak, neighbors
gone stodgy, days that lean casually grunting
and snoring together. For anyone who ever needs
the person they slighted, this is my address: "Gone."

An Archival Print

God snaps your picture—don't look away—
this room right now, your face tilted
exactly as it is before you can think
or control it. Go ahead, let it betray
all the secret emergencies and still hold
that partial disguise you call your character.

Even your lip, they say, the way it curves
or doesn't, or can't decide, will deliver
bales of evidence. The camera, wide open,
stands ready; the exposure is thirty-five years

or so—after that you have become
whatever the veneer is, all the way through.

Now you want to explain. Your mother
was a certain—how to express it?—*influence.*
Yes. And your father, whatever he was,
you couldn't change that. No. And your town
of course had its limits. Go on, keep talking—
Hold it. Don't move. That's you forever.

The Trouble with Reading

When a goat likes a book, the whole book is gone,
and the meaning has to go find an author again.
But when we read, it's just print—deciphering,
like frost on a window: we learn the meaning
but lose what the frost is, and all that world
pressed so desperately behind.

So some time let's discover how the ink
feels, to be clutching all that eternity onto
page after page. But maybe it is better not
to know; ignorance, that wide country,
rewards you just to accept it. You plunge;
it holds you. And you have become a rich darkness.

The Dream of Now

When you wake to the dream of now
from night and its other dream,
you carry day out of the dark
like a flame.

When spring comes north, and flowers
unfold from earth and its even sleep,

you lift summer on with your breath
lest it be lost ever so deep.

Your life you live by the light you find
and follow it on as well as you can,
carrying through darkness wherever you go
your one little fire that will start again.

Atavism

1

Sometimes in the open you look up
where birds go by, or just nothing,
and wait. A dim feeling comes—
you were like this once: there was air,
and quiet; it was by a lake, or
maybe a river—you were alert
as an otter and were suddenly born
like the evening star into wide
still worlds like this one you have found
again, for a moment, in the open.

2

Something is being told in the woods: aisles of
shadow lead away; a branch waves;
a pencil of sunlight slowly travels its
path. A withheld presence almost
speaks, but then retreats, rustles
a patch of brush. You can feel
the centuries ripple—generations
of wandering, discovering, being lost
and found, eating, dying, being born.
A walk through the forest strokes your fur,
the fur you no longer have. And your gaze
down a forest aisle is a strange, long
plunge, dark eyes looking for home.
For delicious minutes you can feel your whiskers
wider than your mind, away out over everything.

Trying to Tell It

The old have a secret.
They can't tell others, for to understand
you have to be old.

You need that soft velvet over the ears
and the blessing of time in your hands.
Any challenging sound has a bell at the end.

The vista you heard on a phone all your life
has moved into your head,
where it lures you to listen away.

The secret is wrapped in a message you begin
to hear even in silence.
and at night it wakes you and calls.

The secret is told to you by touches
that spread a thin layer of understanding
again and again, a hint, another: conviction.

You can't see it or hear it but it's there,
like a live wire, a power inside things,
an art, a fantasy.

You have always wanted more than the earth;
now you have it. You turn to the young.
They do not understand.

Remarks on My Character

Waving a flag I retreat a long way beyond
any denial, all the way over the scorched earth,
and come into an arching grove of evasions,
onto those easy paths, one leading to another
and covered ever deeper with shade: I'll never
dare the sun again, that I can promise.

It is time to practice the shrug: "Don't count on
me." Or practice the question that drags its broken
wing over the ground and leads into the swamp
where vines trip anyone in a hurry, and a final
dark pool waits for you to stare at yourself
while shadows move closer over your shoulder.

That's my natural place; I can live where the blurred
faces peer back at me. I like the way
they blend, and no one is ever sure of itself
or likely to settle in unless you scare off
the others. Afraid but so deep no one can follow,
I steal away there, holding my arms like a tree.

You Don't Know the End

Even as you are dying, a part of the world
can be your own—a badger taught me that,
with its foot in a trap on the bank of the Cimarron.

I offered the end of a stick near the lowered head:
space turned into a dream that other things had,
and four long grooves appeared on that hard wood.

My part that day was to learn. It wasn't folklore
I saw, or what anyone said, when I looked
far, past miles around me:

Wherever I went, a new life had begun,
hidden in grass, or waiting beyond the trees.
There is a spirit abiding in everything.

Different Things

1
Steel hardly knows what a hint is, but for thistledown
all you have to do is breathe. And a patch of new cement
will remember a touch forever.

2
One time I asked Agnes to dance. How she
put up her arms—I thought of that this morning
fifty years later.

3
Salmon return out of a wide ocean
and find their home river all the way back
through the bitter current.

4
Under sequoias, tiny blue flowers, dim
all day and almost invisible, grow out of moss.
They reach deep into night for that color.

The Light by the Barn

The light by the barn that shines all night
pales at dawn when a little breeze comes.

A little breeze comes breathing the fields
from their sleep and waking the slow windmill.

The slow windmill sings the long day
about anguish and loss to the chickens at work.

The little breeze follows the slow windmill
and the chickens at work till the sun goes down—

Then the light by the barn again.

Five A.M.

Still dark, the early morning breathes
a soft sound above the fire. Hooded
lights on porches lead past lawns,
a hedge; I pass the house of the couple
who have the baby, the yard with the little
dog; my feet pad and grit on the pavement, flicker
past streetlights; my arms alternate
easily to my pace. Where are my troubles?

There are people in every country who never
turn into killers, saints have built
sanctuaries on islands and in valleys,
conquerors have quit and gone home, for thousands
of years farmers have worked their fields.
My feet begin the uphill curve
where a thicket spills with birds every spring.
The air doesn't stir. Rain touches my face.

Climbing along the River

Willows never forget how it feels
to be young.

Do you remember where you came from?
Gravel remembers.

Even the upper end of the river
believes in the ocean.

Exactly at midnight
yesterday sighs away.

What I believe is,
all animals have one soul.

Over the land they love
they crisscross forever.

Ground Zero [June 1982]

While we slept—
    rain found us last night, easing in
    from the coast, a few leaves at first,
    then ponds. The quietest person in the state
    heard the mild invasion. Before it was over
    every field knew that benediction.

At breakfast—
    while we talked some birds passed, then slanted
    north, wings emphasizing earth's weight
    but overcoming it. "There's no hope,"
    you said. Our table had some flowers
    cascading color from their vase. Newspapers
    muttered repression and shouted revolution.
    A breeze lifted curtains; they waved
    easily. "Why can't someone do something!"
    My hand began its roving, like those curtains,
    and the flowers bending, and the far-off bird wings.

Network

It shakes whenever you try—the tree by the door
held lightly, those days that stretch out their soft
gray links to each other, mother and father
bound close and the circle of town
alive when a train struggles past. Desolate,
yes, but connected, everything touches
whatever is left. Nobody ever
escapes, or wants to, really: what reaches
out leads back to the center and shivers
long after you're gone. That's why it's home.

For a Lost Child

What happens is, the kind of snow that sweeps
Wyoming comes down while I'm asleep. Dawn
finds our sleeping bag but you are gone.
Nowhere now, you call through every storm,
a voice that wanders without a home.

Across bridges that used to find a shore
you pass, and along shadows of trees that fell
before you were born. You are a memory
too strong to leave this world that slips away
even as its precious time goes on.

I glimpse you often, faithful to every country
we ever found, a bright shadow the sun
forgot one day. On a map of Spain
I find your note left from a trip that year
our family traveled: "Daddy, we could meet here."

Consolations

"The broken part heals even stronger than the rest,"
they say. But that takes awhile.
And, "Hurry up," the whole world says.
They tap their feet. And it still hurts on rainy
afternoons when the same absent sun
gives no sign it will ever come back.

"What difference in a hundred years?"
The barn where Agnes hanged her child
will fall by then, and the scrawled words
erase themselves on the floor where rats' feet
run. Boards curl up. Whole new trees
drink what the rivers bring. Things die.

"No good thing is easy." They told us that,
while we dug our fingers into the stones

and looked beseechingly into their eyes.
They say the hurt is good for you. It makes
what comes later a gift all the more
precious in your bleeding hands.

Security

Tomorrow will have an island. Before night
I always find it. Then on to the next island.
These places hidden in the day separate
and come forward if you beckon.
But you have to know they are there before they exist.

Some time there will be a tomorrow without any island.
So far, I haven't let that happen, but after
I'm gone others may become faithless and careless.
Before them will tumble the wide unbroken sea,
and without any hope they will stare at the horizon.

So to you, Friend, I confide my secret:
to be a discoverer you hold close whatever
you find, and after a while you decide
what it is. Then, secure in where you have been,
you turn to the open sea and let go.

Long Distance

We didn't know at the time. It was
for us, a telephone call through the world
and nobody answered.

We thought it was a train far off
giving its horn, roving its headlight
side to side in its tunnel of darkness
and shaking the bridge and our house
till dishes rattled, and going away.

We thought it a breath climbing the well where Kim
almost fell in; it was a breath saying his name,
and "Almost got you," but we piled boards
and bricks on top and held off that voice.

Or maybe it was the song in the stove—
walnut and elm giving forth stored sunlight
through that narrow glass eye on the front
in the black door that held in the fire.

Or a sigh from under the mound of snow where Bret's
little car with its toy wheels nestled all winter
ready to roll, come spring, and varoom
when his feet toddled it along.

Or—listen—in the cardboard house
we built by the kitchen wall, a doorknob
drawn with crayon, Kit's little window peeking
out by the table—is it a message from there?

And from Aunt Helen's room where she sews
all day on a comforter made out of pieces of Grandma's
dresses, and the suits for church—maybe those
patches rustle their message in her fingers:
"Dorothy, for you, and for all the family I sew
that we may be warm in the house by the tracks."

I don't know, but there was a voice,
those times, a call through the world that almost
rang everywhere, and we looked up—Dorothy, Helen,
Bret, Kim, Kit—and only the snow
shifted its foot outside in the wind,
and nobody heard.

Your Life

You will walk toward the mirror,
closer and closer, then flow
into the glass. You will disappear
some day like that, being
more real, more true, at the last.

You learn what you are, but slowly,
a child, a woman, a man,
a self often shattered, and pieces
put together again till the end:
you halt, the glass opens—

A surface, an image, a past.

Yes

It could happen any time, tornado,
earthquake, Armageddon. It could happen.
Or sunshine, love, salvation.

It could, you know. That's why we wake
and look out—no guarantees
in this life.

But some bonuses, like morning,
like right now, like noon,
like evening.

What's in My Journal

Odd things, like a button drawer. Mean
things, fishhooks, barbs in your hand.
But marbles too. A genius for being agreeable.
Junkyard crucifixes, voluptuous
discards. Space for knickknacks, and for
Alaska. Evidence to hang me, or to beatify.
Clues that lead nowhere, that never connected
anyway. Deliberate obfuscation, the kind
that takes genius. Chasms in character.
Loud omissions. Mornings that yawn above
a new grave. Pages you know exist
but you can't find them. Someone's terribly
inevitable life story, maybe mine.

Merci Beaucoup

It would help if no one ever mentioned
France again. Its words are the ones
that get me most into trouble, especially
naïve and *folie*. Someone sits down
beside me in church and says, "*Bonjour*."
"Likewise," I say, and they look at me.
See what I mean? It's a French look, and I never
get used to that other word they begin to think of.

Or my lady friend says, "*Merci*," and right away
I'm caught up in France, wanting to say "*Adiós*"
but usually saying, "Likewise," as nice as I can
so that she'll see I'm agreeable, no matter
what language we're in. But I can tell she's thinking,
"Far out," the way they say it over there.

Here's the thing—it's not the words, really;
it's being lost from that high ground you have
if you're the one who's the insider. It's the "Mother"

tongue that says, "Be the way I tell you
and you can have my approval but don't ask any questions."
So I don't. I'm back home at the foot of the table
holding the fork right, learning to say, "Likewise."

Young

Before time had a name, when win
or lose were the same, in a forsaken
town I lived unnoticed, blessed.
Remember when shadows played
because there were leaves in the wind?
And people came to our door from a land
where stories were real?
Barefoot, we traveled the roads
all summer. At night we drew pictures
of home with smoke from the chimney.
And we frowned when we read,
so we could understand.

After the years came true, but before
their cost, I played in that big world, too,
and often won: this face was known;
gold came into these hands.
But unwieldy hours overwhelmed
my time. All I intended blew away.
The best of my roads went wrong,
no matter my age, no matter
how long I tried.
It was far, it was dim,
toward the last. And nobody knew how
heavy it was by the end,
for that same being who lived back then.

Don't you see how it was, for a child?
Don't you understand?

Life Work

Even now in my hands the feel of the shovel comes back,
the shock of gravel or sand. Sun-scorch on my shoulders
bears down. The boss is walking around barking.
All the cement mixers rattle and jolt.

That day the trench we are digging goes deeper
and deeper, over my head; then the earth heaves
in one giant coffin gulp. They keep
digging and pulling and haul me out still breathing.

The sky, right there, was a precious cobalt dome
so near it pressed on my face. Beside me my hands
lay twitching and begging at the end of my arms.
Nothing is far anymore, after that trench, the stones. . . .

Oh near, and blessing again and again: my breath.
And the sky, and steady against my back, the earth.

In Camp

That winter of the war, every day
sprang outward. I was a prisoner.
Somone brought me gifts. That year
now is far: birds can't fly
the miles to find a forgotten cause.

No task I do today has justice
at the end. All I know is
my degree of leaning in this wind
where—once the mind springs free—
every cause has reason
but reason has no law.

In camps like that, if I should go again,
I'd still study the gospel and play the accordion.

Something to Declare

They have never had a war big enough
to slow that pulse in the earth under
our path near that old river.

Even as a swallow swims through the air
a certain day skips and returns, hungry for
the feel and lift of the time passed by.

That was the place where I lived awhile
dragging a wing, and the spin of the world
started its tilt into where it is now.

They say that history is going on somewhere.
They say it won't stop. I have held
one picture still for a long time and waited.

This is only a little report floated
into the slow current so the wind will know
which way to come if it wants to find me.

How These Words Happened

In winter, in the dark hours, when others
were asleep, I found these words and put them
together by their appetites and respect for
each other. In stillness, they jostled. They traded
meanings while pretending to have only one.

Monstrous alliances never dreamed of before
began. Sometimes they last. Never again
do they separate in this world. They die
together. They have a fidelity that no
purpose or pretense can ever break.

And all this happens like magic to the words
in those dark hours when others sleep.

The Size of a Fist

This engine started years ago—many—,
small heart pounding, lungs gasping,
reaching for air, fist curled and ready,
all those months and the subtle tides: nursery,
the schoolground terror, engine beat-beat,
work in the fields, hoe, shovel, wheelbarrow,
engine steady, then on through rooms, faces
grim, turned aside often, beat, move on,
beat, late at night, where? where rest?
even today—who is this old guy?—,
beat, beat, engine cruising, day, night,
beat and away.

Vita

God guided my hand
and it wrote,
"Forget my name."

World, please note—
a life went by, just
a life, no claims,

A stutter in the millions
of stars that pass,
a voice that lulled—

A glance
and a world
and a hand.

Editing This Book: An Afterword

THIS VOLUME was made from some three thousand poems published by William Stafford either in journals or in the sixty-seven volumes from *West of Your City* (1960) to *Even in Quiet Places* (1996), and from the poet's Daily Writings, with special attention to those of the last year of his life. The gathering of materials and the first selection (down to about five hundred poems) was the responsibility of the staff of the William Stafford Archive: Diane McDevitt, Paul Merchant, and Vincent Wixon, led by Kim Stafford.

The selection was further refined through correspondence with a number of friends of Stafford's poetry and was completed in consultation with Fiona McCrae and her staff at Graywolf Press, notably Fred Marchant. The editors are especially grateful to Robert Bly and Naomi Shihab Nye for their generous donation of time and goodwill to the project, and to Tom Andrews, Marvin Bell, Jonathan Holden, Judith Kitchen, Linda Pastan, and Jarold Ramsey, who as generously shared expertise and offered encouragement in response to our ideas.

These various responses to the first selection reminded the editors how directly this poet engages with his audience. For each reader, it seems, there is a different William Stafford, one who is tougher, more philosophical, more genial, more inclined to reminiscence, lighter, softer, or darker than other William Staffords. He is, of course, all of these, and to represent all of them fully would have taken a volume of twice this size. The editors have attempted to provide characteristic examples of each of the poet's many voices and strategies, from every stage of his career.

The volume is organized as follows: recent poems in the first section; a second section selected from the six volumes collected by HarperCollins in *Stories That Could Be True* (1977); a third section of poems published by other publishers, mostly in limited editions; and a fourth section selected from the poet's last three HarperCollins volumes, *A Glass Face in the Rain, An Oregon Message,* and *Passwords.*

The late poems in the first section are presented in two parts: the first, subtitled *Sometimes I Breathe*, is based on a book manuscript left for publication by the poet; the second part, *There's a Thread You Follow*, has been selected from William Stafford's poems written between January 1993 and his death in August of the same year, and ends with the poem written on his last morning.

Index of Titles

Index of First Lines

William Edgar Stafford (1914-1993) was born in Hutchinson, Kansas. In his early years he worked a variety of jobs—in sugar beet fields, in construction, at an oil refinery—and received his bachelor's and master's degrees from the University of Kansas. A conscientious objector and pacifist, he spent the years 1942-46 in Arkansas and California work camps, fighting forest fires, building and maintaining trails and roads, and halting soil erosion. After the war he taught high school, worked for Church World Service, and joined the English faculty of Lewis & Clark College in Portland, where (with time out for earning a PhD from the University of Iowa) he taught until his retirement. Married to Dorothy Hope Frantz in 1944, the father of four children, Stafford authored 67 volumes, the first of which, *West of Your City*, was published when he was 46. In addition to the 1963 National Book Award for *Traveling through the Dark*, Stafford's many honors included Poetry Consultant for the Library of Congress (1970-71) and the Shelley Award from the Poetry Society of America. He was appointed Oregon Poet Laureate in 1975. An enormously loved and admired writer, a generous mentor to aspiring poets everywhere, Stafford traveled thousands of miles in his later years, giving hundreds of readings in colleges and universities, community centers and libraries, throughout the United States and in Egypt, India, Bangladesh, Pakistan, Iran, Germany, Austria, and Poland.

The Way It Is has been produced for Graywolf Press at Stanton Publication Services, Inc., in Saint Paul, Minnesota. The typeface is Legacy, designed by Ron Arnholm. Legacy reinterprets Renaissance masterpieces for digital composition. The roman is based on a type cut in Venice by Nicolas Jenson around 1469. The italic is based on letters cut in Paris by Claude Garamond around 1539. This book was designed by Will Powers and has been printed on acid-free paper by Maple Vail Book Manufacturing.